Around The Word In 121 Days

Suzanne Wright

Dedication

I want to dedicate this devotional book to my three children, Nathanael Wright, Jonathan Wright and Christyn Carter. You have always encouraged me and been a source of strength to me. You have always believed in me and made me feel that I could accomplish anything. Through so many trials, through so much loss and through so much pain in my life, you have stood by me.

I am so thankful to God for blessing me with such amazing, thoughtful, giving and kind children. Thank you for never being afraid to speak truth into my life. I am a better person because of all of you.

Love you forever,

Mom

Acknowledgment

My life was falling apart. I had gone through so much hurt and pain in my life, that I didn't know how I would continue. I needed more, more of the Lord, more community, more truth. I started attending Crossroads Bible Church in Ingersol Ontario and my life was drastically changed. The first six weeks, I attended Crossroads Church, I sat there and cried through the worship service and cried through the message and then left as soon as the service was over. God used the worship and the word to bring healing into my heart and into my life. Every week, the Worship brought me to the throne room of the Lord, and the Word fed me, healed me and taught me truth that I had never heard before. After the initial six weeks, God started using the community to continue the healing process. I started meeting people and I started sticking around. and the Community gave me a sense of belonging and love. I no longer felt like I was alone, I no longer felt empty.

God used the pain in my life to bring me closer to Him and He used Crossroads as the vessel to make that happen.

Contents

Dedication iii

Acknowledgment iv

Why This Challenge? xxx

Day 1 1

    Read Genesis 1 to Genesis 12 1

    Memorize 3

    Prayer 3

Day 2 4

    Read Genesis 13 to Genesis 24 4

    Memorize 5

    Prayer 5

Day 3 6

    Read Genesis 25 to Genesis 33 6

    Memorize 7

    Prayer 8

Day 4 9

    Read Genesis 34 to Genesis 43 9

Memorize 10

Prayer 11

Day 5 12

Read Genesis 44 to Exodus 3................................. 12

Memorize 13

Prayer 14

Day 6 15

Read Exodus 4 to Exodus 12 15

Memorize 16

Prayer 16

Day 7 17

Day 8 18

Read Exodus 13 to Exodus 24 18

Memorize 19

Prayer 19

Day 9 21

Read Exodus 25 to Exodus 34 21

Memorize 22

Prayer 22

Day 10 23

    Read Exodus 35 to Leviticus 6 23

    Memorize 24

    Prayer 24

Day 11 26

    Read Leviticus 7 – Leviticus 15................................... 26

    Memorize 27

    Prayer 27

Day 12 28

    Read Leviticus 16 to Leviticus 25 28

    Memorize 30

    Prayer 30

Day 13 31

    Read Leviticus 26 – Numbers 6................................... 31

    Memorize 32

    Prayer 32

Day 14 33

Day 15 34

    Read Numbers 7 – Numbers 16 34

Memorize 36

Prayer 36

Day 16 37

Read Numbers 17 to Numbers 26 37

Memorize 38

Prayer 38

Day 17 39

Read Numbers 27 to Numbers 36 39

Memorize 40

Prayer 41

Day 18 42

Read Deuteronomy 1 to Deuteronomy 13 42

Memorize 43

Prayer 43

Day 19 44

Read Deuteronomy 14 to Deuteronomy 25 44

Memorize 45

Prayer 45

Day 20 46

Read Deuteronomy 26 to Joshua 3 46

Memorize 47

Prayer 47

Day 21 48

Day 22 49

Read Joshua 4 – Joshua 13.................................... 49

Memorize 50

Prayer 50

Day 23 51

Read Joshua 14 – Joshua 22.................................. 51

Memorize 52

Prayer 53

Day 24 54

Read Joshua 23 to Judges 6 54

Memorize 55

Prayer 55

Day 25 56

Read Judges 7 to Judges 15 56

Memorize 57

Prayer 58

Day 26 59

Read Judges 16 to 1 Samuel 2 59

Memorize 60

Prayer 60

Day 27 61

Read 1 Samuel 3 to 1 Samuel 11 61

Memorize 62

Prayer 62

Day 28 63

Day 29 64

Read 1 Samuel 12 to 1 Samuel 19 64

Memorize 65

Prayer 65

Day 30 66

Read 1 Samuel 20 to 1 Samuel 29 66

Memorize 67

Prayer 67

Day 31 69

Read 1 Samuel 30 to 2 Samuel 9 69

Memorize 70

Prayer 71

Day 32 72

Read 2 Samuel 10 to 2 Samuel 17 72

Memorize 73

Prayer 73

Day 33 74

Read 2 Samuel 18 to 2 Samuel 24 74

Memorize 75

Prayer 75

Day 34 76

Read 1 Kings 1 – 1 Kings 7 76

Memorize 77

Prayer 77

Day 35 78

Day 36 79

Read 1 Kings 8 to 1 Kings 14 79

Memorize 80

Prayer 80

Day 37 81

    Read 1 Kings 15 to 1 Kings 21 81

    Memorize 82

    Prayer 82

Day 38 83

    Read 1 Kings 22 to 2 Kings 7 83

    Memorize 84

    Prayer 84

Day 39 85

    Read 2 Kings 8 to 2 Kings 15 85

    Memorize 86

    Prayer 86

Day 40 87

    Read 2 Kings 16 to 2 Kings 23 87

    Memorize 88

    Prayer 89

Day 41 90

    Read 2 Kings 24 to 1 Chronicles 7 90

Memorize 91

Prayer 91

Day 42 92

Day 43 93

Read 1 Chronicles 8 to 1 Chronicles 16.................................... 93

Memorize 95

Prayer 95

Day 44 96

Read 1 Chronicles 17 to 1 Chronicles 24................................... 96

Memorize 97

Prayer 97

Day 45 98

Read 1 Chronicles 25 to 2 Chronicles 6.................................... 98

Memorize 99

Prayer 99

Day 46 100

Read 2 Chronicles 7 to 2 Chronicles 18................................... 100

Memorize 101

Prayer 101

Day 47 102

    Read 2 Chronicles 19 to 2 Chronicles 31 102

    Memorize 103

    Prayer 104

Day 48 105

    Read 2 Chronicles 32 to Ezra 3 105

    Memorize 106

    Prayer 106

Day 49 107

Day 50 108

    Read Ezra 4 to Ezra 10 108

    Memorize 109

    Prayer 109

Day 51 110

    Read Nehemiah 1 to Nehemiah 9 110

    Memorize 111

    Prayer 112

Day 52 113

    Read Nehemiah 10 to Esther 10 113

Memorize 114

Prayer 114

Day 53 116

Read Job 1 to Job 12 116

Memorize 117

Prayer 117

Day 54 118

Read Job 13 to Job 27 118

Memorize 119

Prayer 119

Day 55 120

Read Job 28 to Job 40 120

Memorize 121

Prayer 121

Day 56 122

Day 57 123

Read Job 41 to Psalm 10 123

Memorize 124

Prayer 124

Day 58 125

    Read Psalm 11 to Psalm 27 125

    Memorize 126

    Prayer 127

Day 59 128

    Read Psalm 28 to Psalm 44 128

    Memorize 129

    Prayer 130

Day 60 131

    Read Psalm 45 to Psalm 69 131

    Memorize 132

    Prayer 132

Day 61 133

    Read Psalm 70 to Psalm 80 133

    Memorize 134

    Prayer 134

Day 62 135

    Read Psalm 81 to Psalm 96 135

    Memorize 136

Prayer 136

Day 63 137

Memorize 137

Day 64 138

Read Psalm 97 to Psalm 113 138

Memorize 139

Prayer 139

Day 65 140

Read Psalm 114 to Psalm 119 140

Memorize 141

Prayer 141

Day 66 142

Read Psalm 120 to Psalm 137 142

Memorize 143

Prayer 143

Day 67 144

Read Psalm 138 to Proverbs 5 144

Memorize 145

Prayer 146

Day 68 147

    Read Proverbs 6 to 17 147

    Memorize 148

    Prayer 148

Day 69 149

    Read Proverbs 18 to31 149

    Memorize 150

    Prayer 150

Day 70 151

    Memorize 151

Day 71 152

    Read Ecclesiastes 1 to Ecclesiastes 12..................... 152

    Memorize 153

    Prayer 154

Day 72 155

    Read Song of Solomon 1 to Isaiah 6......................... 155

    Memorize 156

    Prayer 157

Day 73 158

Read Isaiah 7 to Isaiah 20 158

Memorize 159

Prayer 159

Day 74 160

Read Isaiah 21 to Isaiah 32 160

Memorize 161

Prayer 161

Day 75 162

Read Isaiah 33 to Isaiah 44 162

Memorize 163

Prayer 163

Day 76 164

Read Isaiah 45 to Isaiah 54 164

Memorize 165

Prayer 165

Day 77 166

Memorize 166

Day 78 167

Read Isaiah 56 to Isaiah 65 167

Memorize 168

Prayer 168

Day 79 169

Read Isaiah 66 to Jeremiah 8 169

Memorize 170

Prayer 170

Day 80 171

Read Jeremiah 9 to Jeremiah 17 171

Memorize 172

Prayer 172

Day 81 173

Read Jeremiah 18 to Jeremiah 28 173

Memorize 174

Prayer 174

Day 82 175

Read Jeremiah 29 to Jeremiah 40 175

Memorize 176

Prayer 176

Day 83 177

Read Jeremiah 41 to Jeremiah 48 177

Memorize 178

Prayer 178

Day 84 179

Day 85 180

Read Jeremiah 49 to Lamentations 5 180

Memorize 181

Prayer 181

Day 86 182

Read Ezekiel 1 to Ezekiel 12 182

Memorize 183

Prayer 184

Day 87 185

Read Ezekiel 13 to Ezekiel 18 185

Memorize 186

Prayer 186

Day 88 187

Read Ezekiel 19 to Ezekiel 26 187

Memorize 188

Prayer 188

Day 89 189

    Read 189

    Ezekiel 27 to Ezekiel 37 189

    Memorize 190

    Prayer 190

Day 90 191

    Read Ezekiel 38 to Ezekiel 46 191

    Memorize 192

    Prayer 192

Day 91 193

    Memorize 193

Day 92 194

    Read Ezekiel 47 to Daniel 5.................. 194

    Memorize 196

    Prayer 196

Day 93 197

    Read Daniel 6 to Hosea 6...................... 197

    Memorize 199

Prayer 199

Day 94 200

Read Hosea 6 to Amos 3 200

Memorize 201

Prayer 201

Day 95 202

Read Amos 4 to Jonah 4 202

Memorize 204

Prayer 204

Day 96 205

Read Micah 1 to Habakkuk 3 205

Memorize 206

Prayer 206

Day 97 207

Read Zephaniah 1 to Zechariah 9 207

Memorize 208

Prayer 208

Day 98 209

Memorize 209

Day 99 210

    Read Zechariah 10 to Malachi 4 210

    Memorize 211

    Prayer 211

Day 100 212

    Read Matthew 1 to Matthew 10 212

    Memorize 213

    Prayer 213

Day 101 214

    Read Matthew 11 to Matthew 20 214

    Memorize 215

    Prayer 215

Day 102 216

    Read Matthew 21 to Matthew 28 216

    Memorize 217

    Prayer 218

Day 103 219

    Read Mark 1 to Mark 8 219

    Memorize 220

Prayer 220

Day 104 221

    Read Mark 9 to Luke 6 221

    Memorize 222

    Prayer 223

Day 105 224

    Memorize 224

Day 106 225

    Read Luke 7 to Luke 18 225

    Memorize 226

    Prayer 226

Day 107 227

    Read Luke 19 to John 2 227

    Memorize 228

    Prayer 228

Day 108 229

    Read John 3 to John 11 229

    Memorize 230

    Prayer 230

Day 109..231

    Read John 12 to Acts 2 231

    Memorize 232

    Prayer 232

Day 110..234

    Read Acts 3 to Acts 15... 234

    Memorize 235

    Prayer 235

Day 111..236

    Read Acts 16 to Acts 28....................................... 236

    Memorize 238

    Prayer 238

Day 112..239

    Memorize 239

Day 113..240

    Read Romans 1 to Romans 16 240

    Memorize 241

    Prayer 241

Day 114..242

Read 1 Corinthians 1 to 1 Corinthians 15 242

Memorize 243

Prayer 243

Day 115 244

Read 1 Corinthians 16 to 2 Corinthians 13 244

Memorize 245

Prayer 245

Day 116 246

Read Galatians 1 to Philippians 4 246

Memorize 247

Prayer 248

Day 117 249

Read Colossians 1 to 1 Timothy 2 249

Memorize 250

Prayer 250

Day 118 251

Read 1 Timothy 3 to Hebrews 4 251

Memorize 252

Prayer 252

Day 119...253

    Read Hebrews 5 to 1 Peter 1.................................... 253

    Memorize 255

    Prayer 255

Day 120...256

    Read 1 Peter 2 to Revelation 3................................ 256

    Memorize 257

    Prayer 257

Day 121...258

    Read Revelation 4 to Revelation 22......................... 258

    Memorize 259

    Prayer 259

About The Author...260

Page Blank Intentionally

Why This Challenge?

A few months ago, I heard our Pastor pray, as he does every Sunday, "LORD, we love you and we love your word". Although I have heard him pray this every week, this particular week, it struck me. I love the LORD, but do I love His word? I read it, in fact for years now, I have been reading through the bible every year, and just to let you know, that is 3.4 chapters in the bible per day.

So, for years now, I have been reading 3.4 chapters per day. Sometimes that would take me as much as 15 minutes per day, but if they are short chapters, it might take me as little as 5 minutes per day. For the first time, I questioned my love for the LORD's word.

Then one other Sunday, our Pastor mentioned reading God's word like an entire story, to help it make sense. Well for months before all of this, I had been asking the LORD to help me to understand His word so that I am able to answer the questions that people ask me.

Then it hit me, God was answering my prayer. He was showing me how to understand His word and was teaching me how to answer the questions that people ask me. I was to fall in love with his word. We don't fall in love by spending 5 to 15 minutes a day with someone, therefore, I had to read His word more aggressively.

So, every day before I would start reading, I prayed and

asked the LORD to help me retain His word, help me to understand His word, and meet me through His word. Since then, I have been reading through the bible several times.

I want to put a challenge out there to anyone who wants to accept it. Try to read through the bible in 121 days, that's four months. It takes less than one hour out of your day to follow this study guide. I have added some of my own thoughts to help us get something out of it each day.

Most of us waste at least an hour a day, either on social media or by watching our favorite TV shows or movies or reading fictional books. I am naming these because some of these are my time wasters. I love reading fiction, I love watching Hallmark movies, and I'm not on social media much, maybe ten minutes per day, but I do have a game I love to play on my tablet that could easily waste an hour a day if I let it.

For those with young children, I understand your time constraints. I had three young children at one time, and just spending any time with the LORD each day was a challenge. I didn't home-school my children, but I did volunteer at their school so that I could have input in their daily education. Some of the things I did to ensure that I spent time with the LORD every day asking my husband for the time at night (asking him to fold the laundry or do the dishes) so that I could spend time with the LORD. I would get up before my children to pray. (My children often caught their mother in prayer in the morning – definitely not a bad thing to get caught doing). I would take long baths with my bible.

Here are some ideas for busy moms, listen to the word audibly, ask your spouse for help, and read the word to your children before they go to bed at night. Or here is a thought, ask the LORD to help you find the time.

I have also added a memory verse, one per week to make it easier for us. The Bible says, "I hide your Word in my heart so I might not sin against you," Psalm 119:11. By memorizing verses in the bible, they are there when we need them. We don't always have a bible handy, but we can have His Word handy if we hide it in our hearts.

You can do all of this alone or find someone to take this challenge with and encourage each other holding each other accountable. Or you can take this idea and do your own thing. I just want to challenge you to do something.

God has used prayer, personal struggles, and His word to bring me to a place of having a strong devotional life.

I hope you will join us, or at the very least do your own thing to read God's word more.

Have Fun,

Suzanne Wright

Day 1

Read

Genesis 1 to Genesis 12

When we start reading the Bible, we recognize that God had a plan all along. I love how the attributes of God are so prevalent when reading about creation.

God is Sovereign: (He has the right to exercise His ruling power over His creation – *Genesis 1:1*)

God is Omnipresent: (There is no beginning or end to God, He always was – *Genesis 1:1*)

God is Omniscient: (God knows everything, nothing can be hidden from Him – *Genesis 3:9*)

God is Just (He must punish sin and bring about Justice – *Genesis 3:16 and 17*)

God is Merciful (God shows mercy to the sinner – *Genesis 3:21*)

God is loving, God is kind, God is Faithful… there are so many attributes of God, that they cannot be numbered.

I heard a story about an anchor. Boats need anchors to keep them in one place, but the person went on to say that in the midst of a storm, a boat needs 2 anchors; one anchor alone would cause the boat to go around and around, but the two anchors help the boat stay in place during the storm.

I have chosen the two attributes of God that mean the most to me, to be my anchor during the times of trials in my life and to help me to hold firm to the LORD. My two attributes (or in other words, anchors) are that God is Sovereign and that He Loves me.

During difficult times in my life, I would remember that God is Sovereign and that He loves me, therefore, whatever God is allowing me to go through in my life, I could handle it, because in God's Sovereignty, He has allowed these things, and knowing that He loves me, I know that nothing I am going through, whatever it is, is not trivial. God has a purpose for every situation or circumstance that I am going through.

Therefore, I can handle the trials or the storms. There are so many other attributes of God other than God is Sovereign (He is in complete control) and God is love (He loves unconditionally); some of which are, God is Infinite (He is without origin), God is Immutable (He never changes); God is Omniscient (He is all knowing), God is Faithful (He is True), God is Just (He is Righteous), God is Omnipresent (He is everywhere always), God is Omnipotent (He is all Powerful), God is Holy (He is Perfect), God is Merciful (He is compassionate). There are so many more attributes to choose from to be anchors in your life.

When you are going through various trials, what do you hang on to?

Don't wait until you are going through those trials to figure out what you should be hanging on to. Choose your two anchors so that when your storm comes, you have something to hold the boat steady.

Memorize

"And God said, "Let us make man in our image, after our likeness: and let them have dominion over the fish of the sea and over the fowl of the air and over the cattle and over all the earth and over every creeping thing that creepeth on the earth." So, God created man in his own image, in the image of God created he him; male and female created he them.

Genesis 1:26-27 KJV

Prayer

Lord, I love you and I love your word. Help me to fall more deeply in love with you and help me as I read today, to retain and understand what I am reading. I pray that you will speak to me through your word today and in this time of devotion.

Day 2

Read

Genesis 13 to Genesis 24

"Then Abram said to Lot, 'Let there be no strife between you and me, and between your herdsmen and my herdsmen, for we are kinsmen. Is not the whole land before you? Separate yourself from me. If you take the left hand, then I will go to the right, or if you take the right hand, then I will go to the left.'" – *Genesis 13:8-9*

The land was not big enough for Abram and Lot, and their herdsmen were fighting, therefore, Abram knew that the two companies had to separate. Abram, being the man who trusted God that he was, allowed Lot to choose first where he wanted to live. He told Lot, if you choose to go left, I will go right, if you choose to go right, I will go left. Lot chose the lush land of the Jordan Valley, which was well watered as scripture says.

So, Lot packed up his kin and travelled east. Abram was okay with that because he trusted God that where he was, God would cause him to prosper. Abram didn't want to go his own way, he wanted to be led by God. Abram settled in the land of Canaan. What an amazing place to be in our relationship with God. To be able to trust God and say, "God I want to go where you want me to go, do what you want me to do, and be who you want me to be."

And then when Abram did go God's way, God spoke to him and said to look up in the sky from where you are, north, south, east, and west, and I will give this all to you and your offspring forever.

God always has a purpose for what He wants to do in our lives when we give everything over into His hands. Is there something you need to give over to the LORD and trust him with in your life?

Memorize

"And God said, "Let us make man in our image, after our likeness: and let them have dominion over the fish of the sea and over the fowl of the air and over the cattle and over all the earth and over every creeping thing that creepeth on the earth." So, God created man in his own image, in the image of God created he him; male and female created he them.

Genesis 1:26-27 KJV

Prayer

Lord, I love you and I love your word. Help me to fall more deeply in love with you and help me as I read today, to retain and understand what I am reading. I pray that you will speak to me through your word today and in this time of devotion.

Day 3

Read

Genesis 25 to Genesis 33

Now Jacob heard that the sons of Laban were saying, "Jacob has taken all that was our father's, and from what was our father's he has gained all this wealth." The Jacob became angry and berated Laban. Jacob said to Laban, "What is my offense? What is my sin, that you have hotly pursued me?

For you have felt through all my goods; what have you found of all your household goods? Set it here before my kinsmen and your kinsmen, that they may decide between us two.

In these twenty years, I have been with you. Your ewes and your female goats have not miscarried, and I have not eaten the rams of your flocks… These twenty years I have been in your house. I served you fourteen years for your two daughters, and six years for your flock, and you have changed my wages ten times. – *Genesis 31: 1 & 36-37 & 41*

Esau was cheated by his brother Jacob, Jacob was cheated by his Uncle Laban, and Joseph was hurt by his brothers. I love what Joseph says to his brothers when he met up with them again, what you planned for God, God meant for good.

Romans 8:28 reminds us that everything works out for our good when we love the LORD and are called according to His purpose. There are so many times in our lives when we feel cheated and hurt by others. Many times, our hurts come from those who mean the most to us. We know that God is Sovereign, and if He is Sovereign, then we know that He brings about the trials in our lives for our good and for His Glory.

We pray and ask God to do things in our lives. During one of our Sunday sermons, Pastor said that God always answers… Sometimes it is No, that's not good for you, sometimes it is Yes, you are ready for that, and sometimes it is not yet, I want to give it to you, but you can't handle this gift yet, therefore there are things you need to go through to make you ready to receive this gift.

What are some things you are praying for, what might be some reasons why God is saying, not yet? Has the LORD ever asked a hard ask of you? How did you react?

Memorize

"And God said, "Let us make man in our image, after our likeness: and let them have dominion over the fish of the sea and over the fowl of the air and over the cattle and over all the earth and over every creeping thing that creepeth on the earth." So, God created man in his own image, in the image of God created he him; male and female created he them.

Genesis 1:26-27 KJV

7

Prayer

Lord, I love you and I love your word. Help me to fall more deeply in love with you and help me as I read today, to retain and understand what I am reading. I pray that you will speak to me through your word today and in this time of devotion.

Day 4

Read

Genesis 34 to Genesis 43

And God said to him, "I am God Almighty: be fruitful and multiply. A nation and a company of nations shall come from you, and kings shall come from your own body. The land that I gave to Abraham and Isaac I will give to you, and I will give the land to your offspring after you." Then God went up from him to the place where he had spoken with him. And Jacob set up a pillar in the place where he had spoken with him, a pillar of stone. He poured out a drink offering on it and poured oil on it. So, Jacob called the name of the place where God had spoken with him, Bethel. – *Genesis 35:11-15*

Earlier in the chapter, God told Jacob to make an altar to Him, and Jacob told his household to put away their household gods and to purify themselves. Jacob didn't ask his household if they had household gods, he knew they did and told them to get rid of them. Up to this point, Jacob was living on his father's and grandfather's promise from the LORD, but now, God was speaking directly to Jacob, he told him that kings would come from his own body.

He told him that the land that he promised to Abraham and to Isaac, was given to him and his offspring. And Jacob did what God told him to do, he built an altar and called the name of the place, Bethel, which means "House of God". Jacob was no longer relying on the relationship that his father had with God, or the relationship that his grandfather had with God, Jacob had now encountered God himself, and he finally had his own relationship with God; He had his own covenant with God.

Even though God uses people in our lives to draw us to Him, there comes a time in each of our lives when we have to make the decision to follow the LORD not because our parents do, and not because our friends do, we need to have our own relationship with the LORD and follow Him because we choose to.

I was so thankful for the people God used in my life to draw me to Himself to make the decision to make Him the LORD of my life. Since then, I have asked the LORD to use me to do the same for others.

Is there someone God used in your life to bring you to Himself? Have you thanked them? Is there someone that God has put in your life to use you to make a difference in their life and draw them to making a decision to make Jesus their LORD and Savior? The harvest is plentiful, but the workers are few. Ask the LORD to use you in the harvest of souls.

Memorize

"And God said, "Let us make man in our image, after our likeness:

and let them have dominion over the fish of the sea and over the fowl of the air and over the cattle and over all the earth and over every creeping thing that creepeth on the earth." So, God created man in his own image, in the image of God created he him; male and female created he them.

Genesis 1:26-27 KJV

Prayer

Lord, I love you and I love your word. Help me to fall more deeply in love with you and help me as I read today, to retain and understand what I am reading. I pray that you will speak to me through your word today and in this time of devotion.

Day 5

Read

Genesis 44 to Exodus 3

Moses, Moses! Moses replied, "Here am I" and God said, "Take off your sandals, for the place you are standing is Holy Ground. I am the God of your father, the God of Abraham, the God of Isaac, and the God of Jacob." What an introduction. Exodus

Moses was brought up in the household of Pharoah. He wasn't brought up with the Israelites. He knew that he was kin to them, and because he was "adopted", I am sure he heard stories and was curious about the Israelites (after all, he did protect an Israelite by killing an Egyptian), but he didn't really know them.

So, God decided to introduce Himself to Moses. "Moses, Moses!" Imagine you are at your job, minding your own business and then you see the photocopier on fire and a voice coming out of it. That's kind of how Moses must have felt, only it was a burning bush. "Go and tell Pharoah to let my people go".

This is huge. We all experience what we call "burning bush" moments. Those moments when we sense that God is seeking our attention, speaking to us, and calling us to participate in what God is doing in our midst. Burning bush moments change our lives and the lives of those around us. Moses was introduced to God during that "Burning bush" moment and then given an assignment.

Moses was reluctant to accept this assignment and made so many excuses to God. He complained, "I don't speak well, what if they don't listen, send Aaron". God was upset with Moses for his lack of faith and relented by allowing Aaron to walk this journey with Moses, and yet, even though Moses didn't want to do it God's way, God still used him. In fact, God later rebuked Aaron and Marion for speaking against His servant Moses and said "I speak to Moses face to face like a man speaks with his friend" (paraphrase)

What is your assignment? None of us are exempt, we are all called, but what are we called to? Have you figured that out yet? Ask the LORD what it is He is asking you to do. Witness to your co-worker, Help your neighbor? Take some time to pray and ask the LORD for direction in your life. It's okay if you are afraid, Moses was afraid, but God used him to accomplish His will.

Memorize

"And God said, "Let us make man in our image, after our likeness: and let them have dominion over the fish of the sea and over the fowl of the air and over the cattle and over all the earth and over every creeping thing that creepeth on the earth." So, God created man in his own image, in the image of God created he him; male and female created he them.

Genesis 1:26-27 KJV

Prayer

Lord, I love you and I love your word. Help me to fall more deeply in love with you and help me as I read today, to retain and understand what I am reading. I pray that you will speak to me through your word today and in this time of devotion.

Day 6

Read

Exodus 4 to Exodus 12

But Moses said to the LORD, "Oh my LORD, I am not eloquent, either in the past or since you have spoken to your servant, but I am slow of speech and of tongue." Then the LORD said to him, "Who has made man's mouth? Who makes him mute, deaf, or seeing, or blind? Is it not I, the LORD? – *Exodus 4:10-11, ESV*

God is Sovereign. His word says that He formed our inward parts; He knitted us together in our mother's womb. We praise Him, for we are fearfully and wonderfully made. It also says that when I was being made, His eyes saw my unformed substance and in his book were written all of our days, before we were even born. *(Psalm 139).*

God made us exactly how he planned to make us. God told Moses that He is the one who makes man mute, deaf, or seeing or blind. His word says that He created us, every intricate part. He made us perfect with all our imperfections. He chose our family, He chose our intelligence, He gave us our giftings and He gave us our challenges and none of them were trivial. God had a purpose for it all.

Whatever you like or don't like about yourself, God planned you that way. And, He loves you just the way He created you. He is the Potter, we are the clay. He did not make any mistakes. Take a few minutes to thank Him for creating you exactly as you are, for the gifts He gave you, for the challenges He gave you, and for the family He put you in...

Memorize

"And God said, "Let us make man in our image, after our likeness: and let them have dominion over the fish of the sea and over the fowl of the air and over the cattle and over all the earth and over every creeping thing that creepeth on the earth." So, God created man in his own image, in the image of God created he him; male and female created he them.

Genesis 1:26-27 KJV

Prayer

Lord, I love you and I love your word. Help me to fall more deeply in love with you and help me as I read today, to retain and understand what I am reading. I pray that you will speak to me through your word today and in this time of devotion.

Day 7

Spend today catching up on any days that you didn't get finished. It's important to enjoy God's word, and not to get overwhelmed if you fall behind, so today is a catch-up day, or, if you are caught up, it's a good day to spend looking back at what the LORD has spoken to you about, or even spend this hour in prayer. Today is the last day of your memory verse, so you can spend some time with your memory verse.

"And God said, "Let us make man in our image, after our likeness: and let them have dominion over the fish of the sea and over the fowl of the air and over the cattle and over all the earth and over every creeping thing that creepeth on the earth." So, God created man in his own image, in the image of God created he him; male and female created he them.

Genesis 1:26-27 KJV

Day 8

Read

Exodus 13 to Exodus 24

"Fear not, stand firm, and see the salvation of the LORD, which he will work for you today. For the Egyptians whom you see today, you shall never see again. The LORD will fight for you and you have only to be silent." The LORD said to Moses, "Why do you cry to me? Tell the people of Israel to go forward. Lift up your staff and stretch out your hand over the sea and divide it, so that the people of Israel may go through the sea on dry ground. *Exodus 14:13-16*

Our God is a big God and does big things. We tend to focus on the here and now and forget that God has done great things in the past and that He is still doing great things today. The biggest thing God has ever done is to take away every one of our sins, past, present, and future, and if that was all He ever did, that would be enough. But that isn't all He ever did. He designed us, reminding us that we are not a mistake; He sent His Son to die for us, reminding us that we are forgiven; He picked us, reminding us that we are chosen; He redeemed us, reminding us that we are wanted; He showed us grace, reminding us that we are saved; He has a future for us, reminding us that we are children of God!

All that being said, I'll say it again, God is a big God and does big things. There are many trials that we will go through in this world, but we don't have to be afraid, because God has overcome this world. There will always be obstacles in our lives. Some obstacles that you might be going through could be sickness, anxiety, or a bad relationship, but whatever it is, God does not want you to be afraid.

He wants you to stand firm and see the salvation of the LORD. God wants you to have the courage to walk through on dry ground. You may not be able to do it alone, but the bible says that God will never leave you or forsake you *(Hebrews 13:5)*.

Is there an obstacle in your life right now, that you need the LORD to help you overcome? Ask him for strength and courage. Lift up your staff stretch out your hand over the sea and watch God divide it.

Memorize

"The LORD is my strength and my song, and he has become my salvation; he is my God, and I will prepare him a habitation; my father's God, and I will exalt him."

Exodus 15:2 KJV

Prayer

Lord, I love you and I love your word. Help me to fall more deeply in love with you and help me as I read today, to retain and understand what I am reading. I pray that you will speak to me through your word today and in this time of devotion.

Day 9

Read

Exodus 25 to Exodus 34

So, Aaron said to them, "Take off you rings of gold that are in the ears of your wives, your sons, and your daughters, and bring them to me." So, all the people took off the rings of gold that were in their ears and brought them to Aaron. And he received the gold from their hand and fashioned it with a graving tool and made a golden calf. And they said, "These are your gods O Israel, who brought you out of the land of Egypt." *Exodus 32:2-4*

How often do we pray, and God answers that prayer and then He doesn't get the glory? The Israelites were being forced to work as slaves, beaten, and mistreated by the Egyptians, and they cried out to God to save them then when God heard their cries, He answered their prayers and brought the Israelites out of Egypt.

But when everything was taking too much time, they chose to fashion another god, to worship and they actually gave this god credit for bringing them out of Egypt.

Recently, I started a prayer journal in which I put my prayer requests in, and then I put a column in it to put the date that that prayer was answered. I had to do that because so often when God would answer my prayer, (especially if it was answered prayer that took a long time coming), I forgot that I had prayed and asked God for it and that He answered my prayer. I didn't give credit to God.

Take time today to thank God for answered prayer but also thank Him for unanswered prayer, because God's timing is perfect. If you haven't already done so, maybe start a prayer journal, it's a good way to remember when people ask you to pray for them, but it is also a good thing to keep so that you remember to thank God when He does answer your prayers.

Memorize

"The LORD is my strength and my song, and he has become my salvation; he is my God, and I will prepare him a habitation; my father's God, and I will exalt him."

Exodus 15:2 KJV

Prayer

Lord, I love you and I love your word. Help me to fall more deeply in love with you and help me as I read today, to retain and understand what I am reading. I pray that you will speak to me through your word today and in this time of devotion.

Day 10

Read

Exodus 35 to Leviticus 6

The LORD called Moses and spoke to him from the tent of meeting, saying, "Speak to the people of Israel and say to them, when any one of you brings an offering to the LORD, you shall bring your offering to the LORD, you shall bring your offering of livestock from the herd or from the flock". – *Leviticus 1:1-2*

The offerings in the book of Leviticus serve as God's gracious provision for how one could regain fellowship with God. What were the five offerings in Leviticus, and why did they matter? After all, the book of Leviticus was given by God to a people who were already redeemed.

The Burnt Offering teaches that God is pleased to accept anyone who comes to Him through His prescribed sacrifice. The animal is to be consumed on the altar, and it is atoned for the worshipper's sin. God's wrath was satisfied against sin and made fellowship possible between a Holy God and a sinful person.

A Grain Offering was offered to God as a gift from the best of their produce in an act of thanksgiving for their sins being forgiven. The Peace Offering was optional. It was an offering given in addition to the burnt offering. The Peace offering closed with a meal in which the priests, and person offering, and his or her friends ate together. The Purification Offering (or Sin Offering) dealt with 2 issues: forgiveness for unintentional sins and for cleansing from ceremonial uncleanness.

The Guilt Offering had the individual looking beyond their sin to the consequences of their sin. The person not only sought forgiveness but first, he or she paid full restitution. Because the offerings in Leviticus had their ultimate fulfillment in Jesus Christ, there is no need for them today.

When we sin, we need only to go straight to the LORD and ask for forgiveness. Is there anything in your life that you haven't asked the LORD's forgiveness for? It's never too late. Take it to the LORD today.

Memorize

"The LORD is my strength and my song, and he has become my salvation; he is my God, and I will prepare him a habitation; my father's God, and I will exalt him."

Exodus 15:2 KJV

Prayer

Lord, I love you and I love your word. Help me to fall more deeply

in love with you and help me as I read today, to retain and understand what I am reading. I pray that you will speak to me through your word today and in this time of devotion.

Day 11

Read

Leviticus 7 – Leviticus 15

Now Nadab and Abihu, the sons of Aaron, each took his censer and put fire in it and laid incense on it and offered unauthorized fire before the LORD, which he had not commanded them. And fire came out from before the LORD and consumed them, and they died before the LORD. Then Moses said to Aaron, "This is what the LORD has said, "Among those who are near me, I will be sanctified, and before all the people I will be glorified." And Aaron held his peace. – *Leviticus 10: 1-3*

God wants our whole selves. For years, I put other people and other interests before the LORD. I thought that God was first in my life, but it's amazing how things creep in that we put before the LORD. So why were the offerings unauthorized? They disobeyed God's instructions by using "foreign fire" in their sacrifices. They did not comply with the express intent of God.

A similar story happens in Acts when a husband and wife sell their property and give the offering to the church. Had they decided to keep some of it back and let them know that they were only giving a portion, I believe their offering would have been pleasing, had they both not lied and said that this was what they sold their property for (see Acts 5:1-11).

You can't fool God. He is Omniscient, which means He knows all, He wants our offering (our lives) to be a pleasing aroma to Him.

Romans 12:1-2 says "I appeal to you therefore, brothers, by the mercies of God, to present your bodies as a living sacrifice, holy and acceptable to God, which is your spiritual worship. Do not be conformed to this world, but be transformed by the renewal of your mind, that by testing you may discern what is the will of God, what is good and acceptable and perfect.

God wants us to set our affections on things above. He does not just want our sacrifice; He wants our obedience. He wants our hearts.

Memorize

"The LORD is my strength and my song, and he has become my salvation; he is my God, and I will prepare him a habitation; my father's God, and I will exalt him."

Exodus 15:2 KJV

Prayer

Lord, I love you and I love your word. Help me to fall more deeply in love with you and help me as I read today, to retain and understand what I am reading. I pray that you will speak to me through your word today and in this time of devotion.

Day 12

Read

Leviticus 16 to Leviticus 25

And the LORD spoke to Moses, saying, "Speak to all the congregation of the people of Israel and say to them, You shall be holy, for I the LORD your God am holy."

Leviticus 19:1; Every one of you shall revere his mother and his father and you shall keep my Sabbaths: I am the LORD your God.

Leviticus 19:2-3; Do not turn to idols or make for yourselves any gods: I am the LORD your God.

Leviticus 19:4; You shall not steal; you shall not deal falsely; you shall not lie to one another. You shall not swear by my name falsely: I am the LORD.

Leviticus 19:11-12; You shall not hate your brother in your heart, but you shall reason frankly with your neighbor... you shall love your neighbor as yourself: I am the LORD. – *Leviticus 19:17-18*

The 10 Commandments.

We usually remember the big ones like do not steal, do not kill, do not commit adultery. Those are the easiest ones to remember to keep. But how often do we tell a little white lie, talk behind someone's back, or want what others have? The Ten

28

Commandments are not just guidelines.

God gave them to us to guide us and protect us, and to give us a moral code for us to live by. But they were also given to us to show our propensity to sin and to show us our need for a Savior. Unfortunately, we all struggle with sin. The Bible says that we all have sinned *(Romans 3:23)*.

In other words, we all need a savior. Every day, all day. We need the LORD to help make our path straight *(Proverbs 3:6),* We need the LORD to help us make the right decisions and choices. *(James 1:5)*.

Have you acknowledged that you are a sinner? Have you asked the LORD for His forgiveness? Have you recognized your need for a Savior? If you have, wonderful, then you know that you need Him every minute of every day. You know that you cannot live a righteous life and that only because of what Christ did for us through his death, burial, and resurrection are we clothes with the righteousness of Christ. But if you haven't, it's as easy as 1, 2, 3.

1. Acknowledge that you are a sinner.

2. Ask God to forgive you.

3. Recognize your need for a Savior. Write out a prayer to God, thanking Him for everything He is in your life.

Memorize

"The LORD is my strength and my song, and he has become my salvation; he is my God, and I will prepare him a habitation; my father's God, and I will exalt him."

Exodus 15:2 KJV

Prayer

Lord, I love you and I love your word. Help me to fall more deeply in love with you and help me as I read today, to retain and understand what I am reading. I pray that you will speak to me through your word today and in this time of devotion.

Day 13

Read

Leviticus 26 – Numbers 6

"If you walk in my statutes and observe my commandments and do them, then I will give you your rains in their season, and the land shall yield its increase, and the trees of the field shall yield their fruit. Your threshing shall last to the time of the grape harvest, and the grape harvest shall last to the time for sowing.

And you shall eat your bread to the full and dwell in your land securely. I will give peace in the land, and you shall lie down, and none shall make you afraid. And I will remove harmful beasts from the land, and the sword shall not go through your land. You shall chase your enemies, and they shall fall before you by the sword." – *Leviticus 26: 3-7*

God is a good God. In Leviticus, God demonstrates His desire for His people to flourish. God's commandments are meant for His Children's good; they are a means to protect and provide for them. However, since God wants the best for His children, sometimes that means sending rain in their season, and the land yielding its increase and the trees of the field yielding their fruit, but sometimes, it doesn't.

Sometimes, God allows challenges in our lives that bring trials. But no matter what, God always has a purpose and a plan for our lives. When we walk in His statues and serve and love the LORD, everything in our lives, blessings or challenges are always done for our good and for His glory. Blessed be the name of the LORD.

Are there blessings in your life that you have taken for granted? Thank the LORD right now for those blessings. On the other hand, are there trials that you are facing today that you haven't fully given over to the LORD? We are to be joyful when we go through trials, we can only do that if we trust God fully that what we are going through, He will turn around for our good and for His glory.

Memorize

"The LORD is my strength and my song, and he has become my salvation; he is my God, and I will prepare him a habitation; my father's God, and I will exalt him."

Exodus 15:2 KJV

Prayer

Lord, I love you and I love your word. Help me to fall more deeply in love with you and help me as I read today, to retain and understand what I am reading. I pray that you will speak to me through your word today and in this time of devotion.

Day 14

Spend today catching up on any days that you didn't get finished. It's important to enjoy God's word, and not to get overwhelmed if you fall behind, so today is a catch-up day, if you are caught up, it's a good day to spend looking back at what the LORD has spoken to you about, or even spend this hour in prayer. Today is the last day of your memory verse, so you can spend some time with your memory verse.

"The LORD is my strength and my song, and he has become my salvation; he is my God, and I will prepare him a habitation; my father's God, and I will exalt him."

Exodus 15:2 KJV

Day 15

Read

Numbers 7 – Numbers 16

Miriam and Aaron spoke against Moses because of the Cushite woman he had married, for he had married a Cushite woman. And they said, "Has the LORD indeed spoken only through Moses? Has he not spoken through us also?" And the LORD heard it. Now the man Moses was very meek, more than all people who were on the face of the earth. And suddenly the LORD said to Moses and to Aaron and Miriam, "Come out, you three, to the tent of meeting." And the three of them came out.

And the LORD came down in a pillar of cloud and stood at the entrance of the tent and called Aaron and Miriam, and they both came forward. And he said "Hear my words: If there is a prophet among you, I the LORD make myself known to him in a vision; I speak with him in a dream. Not so with my servant Moses. He is faithful in all my house.

With him, I speak mouth to mouth… Why then were you not afraid to speak against my servant Moses? And the anger of the LORD was kindled again them and he departed. – *Numbers 12: 1-9*

Moses' brothers and sisters (Aaron and Miriam) raised some valid points about Moses. Moses teaches the Israelites that they are not to marry foreigners *(Deut 7:3)*, yet he himself married a foreign wife *(Numbers 12:1)*. But they didn't handle it correctly.

They should have gone to Moses to discuss their concerns, but instead, they put themselves in the place of judge and jury and spoke against Moses. Had their complaint not been a pretext to make Moses look bad and revolt against a rebellion in order to place themselves in a higher position, their concerns may have been listened to as valid, but that wasn't their plan. They were causing strife, and strife is so toxic.

God knew that Miriam and Aaron were not as concerned about Moses' marriage in speaking against him as it was that they were causing strife in the camp for their own benefit. It is so important to walk in unity. The bible even says, "If you are laying your gift on the altar and then realize that your brother has something against you, leave your gift and go and make it right." – *Matthew 5:23-24.*

We need to stop strife from entering our realm of influence. It can ruin families, churches, and friends. Have nothing to do with strife. When we speak against others, we are speaking against someone that God created, someone God loves. Someone that God knit together in their mother's womb. God was basically saying to Miriam and Aaron, "How dare you speak again my servant Moses, I created Him, I knit him together, I have counted the hairs on his head, I speak to him face to face."

If you know that you have someone in your life who has strife, take the time to pray and ask the LORD to help you make it right. Don't allow strife to fester, make things right.

Memorize

And the LORD spoke unto Moses, saying, "Speak unto all the congregation of the children of Israel and say unto them, Ye shall be holy, for I the LORD your God am holy."

Leviticus 19:1-2KJV

Prayer

Lord, I love you and I love your word. Help me to fall more deeply in love with you and help me as I read today, to retain and understand what I am reading. I pray that you will speak to me through your word today and in this time of devotion.

Day 16

Read

Numbers 17 to Numbers 26

And the LORD said to Moses, "Make a fiery serpent and set it on a pole, and everyone who is bitten when he sees it, shall live." So, Moses made a bronze serpent and set it on a pole. And if a serpent bit anyone, he would look at the bronze serpent and live. – *Numbers 21:8-9*

Once again, the people complained against Moses and against God, and subsequently, God sent poisonous serpents to punish them. God told Moses to make a serpent and put it on a pole and Moses obeyed God and set a bronze serpent upon the pole.

Bronze typically represents judgment, and a serpent typically represents sin. So having a bronze serpent on a pole is a message to all of us that our sins have been judged. The bronze serpent became salvation from death for anyone who was bitten by the serpents. Just as Jesus became a sin on the cross and the enemy has been defeated. Though the serpent bit the heel of Jesus, Jesus stomped on the head of Satan (the serpent) and crushed Him.

And as Moses lifted up the serpent in the wilderness, even so, the Son of Man must be lifted up so that whoever believed in Him should not perish but have eternal life.

The story of the bronze serpent is a story of hope. Hope that in the midst of suffering, just as the serpent was lifted up, Jesus has been lifted up. We must have the faith to believe in His power.

Jesus became sin on the cross and the enemy has been defeated. The Israelites were grateful for what God provided. We should always be thankful for what God provides. This is a good time to thank God for His goodness in our lives.

Memorize

And the LORD spoke unto Moses, saying, "Speak unto all the congregation of the children of Israel and say unto them, Ye shall be holy, for I the LORD your God am holy."

Leviticus 19:1-2KJV

Prayer

Lord, I love you and I love your word. Help me to fall more deeply in love with you and help me as I read today, to retain and understand what I am reading. I pray that you will speak to me through your word today and in this time of devotion.

Day 17

Read

Numbers 27 to Numbers 36

Moses spoke to the heads of the tribes of the people of Israel saying, "This is what the LORD has commanded. If a man vows a vow to the LORD or swears an oath to bind himself by a pledge, he shall not break his word. He shall do according to all that proceeds out of his mouth." *Numbers 30:1-2*

God has always kept His word, so it's not surprising that it is important that we as well keep our word. When Jesus was preaching the sermon on the mount in Matthew 5, He said, "Let your yes be yes and your no, no; anything more than this comes from the evil one. *Matthew 5:37.*

Too often we make promises that we don't know for sure if we can even keep it. Sometimes it's because we are too busy, something else came up, or let's be honest, maybe it wasn't God's will that we do what we said we would do. But the bible says to let your yes be yes and your no be no, even to your own hurt. It's way too easy to glibly make promises and if something else comes up, we just change our plans.

I've been trying to make my yes, yes and my no, no, and if I have made plans and out of my control, they don't work out, I end up apologizing for not making my yes, yes. One time, I was supposed to babysit my grandson, and I ended up having kidney stones. Anyone who has had them knows how painful they can be.

Anyway, I was unable to be with my grandson, so the next time I saw him, I told him that I was sorry I missed our special day. My grandson knows how important it is to keep your promises, and he said, "That's okay Nana that you broke your promise". Even though I couldn't help it, it made me make the decision to never say yes unless I really mean it.

It is so important that the promises or vows we make are kept, especially the ones we make to the LORD. God takes those commitments seriously. So, the next time you make a commitment, remember how important those commitments are to God. Ask the LORD to help you to keep your promises.

Memorize

And the LORD spoke unto Moses, saying, "Speak unto all the congregation of the children of Israel and say unto them, Ye shall be holy, for I the LORD your God am holy."

Leviticus 19:1-2KJV

Prayer

Lord, I love you and I love your word. Help me to fall more deeply in love with you and help me as I read today, to retain and understand what I am reading. I pray that you will speak to me through your word today and in this time of devotion.

Day 18

Read

Deuteronomy 1 to Deuteronomy 13

"Hear, O Israel: The LORD our God, the LORD is one. You shall love the LORD your God with all your heart and with all your soul and with all your might. And these words that I command you today shall be on our heart. You shall teach them diligently to your children and shall talk of them when you sit in your house, and when you walk by the way, and when you lie down, and when you rise. You shall bind them as a sign on your hand, and they shall be as frontlets between your eyes. You shall write them on the doorposts of your house and on your gates. – *Deuteronomy 6:4-9*

For those who have small children, this is a great scripture to help you know how to share the LORD with your children. The Bible says always. When at the dinner table, when you put them to bed at night, when you go for a walk with them. Always. Putting my children to bed at night was always a wonderful time.

I would sing to them, pray with them, and ask them about their day. We also sat around the table for dinner every night. Families don't sit at the table to eat together as much as they did when I was younger, but they should, that is a great opportunity missed. We used to play High/Low with our children during mealtime.

We would ask them all, "What was your high today?" This was their opportunity to tell us of their accomplishments, then we would say, "What was your low today?" This was their opportunity to share their hurts or challenges. Children need the opportunity to share their day with you, to give them the opportunity to realize how important they are to you and your opportunity to share that with them.

If you aren't already doing this, start a new tradition, start eating together as a family (and not in front of the television), but around a table and talk to each other.

Memorize

And the LORD spoke unto Moses, saying, "Speak unto all the congregation of the children of Israel and say unto them, Ye shall be holy, for I the LORD your God am holy."

Leviticus 19:1-2KJV

Prayer

Lord, I love you and I love your word. Help me to fall more deeply in love with you and help me as I read today, to retain and understand what I am reading. I pray that you will speak to me through your word today and in this time of devotion.

Day 19

Read

Deuteronomy 14 to Deuteronomy 25

"You shall not see your brother's ox or his sheep going astray and ignore them. You shall take them back to your brother. And if he does not live near you and you do not know who he is, you shall bring it home to your house, and it shall stay with you until your brother seeks it. Then you shall restore it to him. And you shall do the same with his donkey or with his garment, or with any lost thing of your brother's, which he loses and you find; you may not ignore it. You shall not see your brother's donkey or his ox fall down by the way and ignore them. You shall help him to lift them up again."

– Deuteronomy 22: 1-4

So much for "Am I my brother's keeper?" Not only are we our brother's keeper, but it seems we are the keeper of the donkey and the ox and sheep as well. Or *Matthew 7:12* puts it another way, do unto others as you would want them to do to them. Also known as the Golden Rule. It doesn't say to do unto others as they do to you, it says as you would want them to do to you.

Just like when Moses encouraged the Israelites to help his brother by looking after his "stuff", we need to think of others more than we think of ourselves. Let's try to live by that Golden Rule.

Deuteronomy 22 teaches that we should not take anything that doesn't belong to us, even if we find them. It's kind of the opposite of that popular says, "finder's keepers, loser's weepers. This chapter is about obeying God and having faith in him. It's also about being our brother's keeper and living by the Golden Rule. If you struggle with putting the needs of others above your own needs, look to Jesus as an example, because when we were sinners, Christ went to the cross and died for us.

Memorize

And the LORD spoke unto Moses, saying, "Speak unto all the congregation of the children of Israel and say unto them, Ye shall be holy, for I the LORD your God am holy."

Leviticus 19:1-2KJV

Prayer

Lord, I love you and I love your word. Help me to fall more deeply in love with you and help me as I read today, to retain and understand what I am reading. I pray that you will speak to me through your word today and in this time of devotion.

Day 20

Read

Deuteronomy 26 to Joshua 3

"And if you faithfully obey the voice of the LORD your God, being careful to do all his commandments that I command you today, the LORD your God will set you high above all the nations of the earth. And all these blessings shall come upon you and overtake you if you obey the voice of the LORD your God. Blessed shall you be in the city, and blessed shall you be in the field. Blessed shall be the fruit of your womb and the fruit of your ground and the fruit of your cattle, the increase of your herds and the young of your flock.

Blessed shall be your basket and kneading bowl. Blessed shall you be when you come in and blessed shall you be when you go out. – *Deuteronomy 28:1-6*

This passage of scripture is a conditional blessing, or promise, if you will. If the Israelites follow the covenants that Moses gave the Israelites, then God's blessing will come upon them and overtake them. God is pretty specific about how He wants to bless His children. I'm not saying that everything always is going to go our way. Let's face it, the bible also says to consider it all joy my brethren when you face various trials. – *James 1:2*.

But here is the thing I want you to get from this, even our trials can be blessings. Everything God does, he does for His glory and for our good. So how can we not call trials, blessings? God said we will be blessed coming in and blessed going out. We don't know what those blessings look like, but when we are thankful, he turns everything around for our good. *Romans 8:28.*

Deuteronomy 28 teaches us about obeying God, it teaches that both blessings and curses happen in our lives. However, if you obey the LORD your God, and keep His commandments, then the LORD your God promises to bless the works of your hands.

Memorize

And the LORD spoke unto Moses, saying, "Speak unto all the congregation of the children of Israel and say unto them, Ye shall be holy, for I the LORD your God am holy."

Leviticus 19:1-2KJV

Prayer

Lord, I love you and I love your word. Help me to fall more deeply in love with you and help me as I read today, to retain and understand what I am reading. I pray that you will speak to me through your word today and in this time of devotion.

Day 21

Spend today catching up on any days that you didn't get finished. It's important to enjoy God's word, and not to get overwhelmed if you fall behind, so today is a catch-up day, if you are caught up, it's a good day to spend looking back at what the LORD has spoken to you about, or even spend this hour in prayer.

Today is the last day of your memory verse, so you can spend some time with your memory verse.

And the LORD spoke unto Moses, saying, "Speak unto all the congregation of the children of Israel and say unto them, Ye shall be holy, for I the LORD your God am holy."

Leviticus 19:1-2KJV

Day 22

Read

Joshua 4 – Joshua 13

When Joshua was by Jericho, he lifted up his eyes and looked, and behold, a man was standing before him with his drawn sword in his hand. And Joshua went to him and said to him, "Are you for us, or for our adversaries? And he said, "No, but I am the commander of the army of the LORD. Now I have come." And Joshua fell on his face to the earth and worshiped and said to him, "What does my LORD say to his servant?" – *Joshua 5:13-14*

God always has a plan. Do you trust God and the plan He has for your life? I finally said to the LORD (after years of a watered-down relationship with Him), "Whatever it takes LORD, I want you to be everything in my life, I want you to be first and to sit on the throne of my heart", and when I said this, everything in my life fell apart. I was in a car accident and live with chronic pain and my marriage fell apart.

But I wanted Him, and I knew that God had a plan. Like Joshua, I essentially said, "What does my LORD say to his servant?" That's what God wants to hear from his children. As difficult as it is to say "Whatever it takes LORD, and as hard as it is to walk through the trials that God allows in our lives to bring us closer to him, I

49

wouldn't give up anything I have gone through because I have far more now than what I lost. God doesn't allow anything in our lives that isn't done for our good and for God's glory.

Are you ready to say to the LORD, "What does my LORD say to his servant?" or in other words, "Whatever it takes LORD" Your life may fall apart (it may not), but God doesn't allow us to go through anything that He doesn't plan for His glory and for our good.

Memorize

"And if it seems evil not you to serve the LORD, Choose you this day whom ye will serve… But as for me and my house, we will serve the LORD."

Joshua 24:15 KJV

Prayer

Lord, I love you and I love your word. Help me to fall more deeply in love with you and help me as I read today, to retain and understand what I am reading. I pray that you will speak to me through your word today and in this time of devotion.

Day 23

Read

Joshua 14 – Joshua 22

Then the LORD said to Joshua, "Tell the Israelites to designate the cities of refuge, as I instructed you through Moses, so that anyone who kills a person accidentally and unintentionally may flee there and find protection from the avenger of blood. When they flee to one of these cities, they are to stand at the entrance of the city gate and state their case before the elders of that city.

Then the elders are to admit the fugitive into their city and provide a place to live among them. If the avenger of blood comes in pursuit, the elders must not surrender the fugitive, because the fugitive killed their neighbor unintentionally and without malice aforethought. They are to stay in that city until they have stood trial before the assembly and until the death of the high priest who is serving at that time. Then they may go back to their own home in the town from which they fled."– *Joshua 20: 1-6 NIV.*

The cities of refuge were Kedesh, Shechem, Hebron, Bezer, Ramoth, and Golan. The law states that anyone who commits murder is to be put to death *(Ex. 21:14),* however, if someone killed someone else by accident, then God in His love for His people, set aside these six cities as an asylum for those murderers.

Basically, Joshua 20 reflects the heart of God. God is a God of justice and mercy and yet He was concerned with those who have simply made mistakes. These cities give reliance on a God who values human life and creates an opportunity to protect the innocent while providing a means for redemption and forgiveness.

It's amazing how often relationships are torn apart because someone made an unintentional mistake. God created a place for people who made serious unintentional mistakes, yet so often we are willing to let those relationships die. Rather than seeking an opportunity to spoon out refuge, we spoon out revenge.

Sometimes it is easier to burn bridges than build them. We too easily allow relationships to fall apart and then work on them. Is there anyone in your life that you have burned bridges with? Is there anyone who God has been speaking to you about restoring your relationship with? Ask God to give you the courage to reach out in restoration.

Memorize

"And if it seems evil not you to serve the LORD, choose you this day whom ye will serve... But as for me and my house, we will serve the LORD."

Joshua 24:15 KJV

Prayer

Lord, I love you and I love your word. Help me to fall more deeply in love with you and help me as I read today, to retain and understand what I am reading. I pray that you will speak to me through your word today and in this time of devotion.

Day 24

Read

Joshua 23 to Judges 6

"Now fear the LORD and serve him with all faithfulness. Throw away the gods your ancestors worshiped beyond the Euphrates River and in Egypt, and serve the LORD. But if serving the LORD seems undesirable to you, then choose for yourselves this day whom you will serve, whether the gods of your ancestors served beyond the Euphrates, or the gods of the Amorites, in whose land you are living. But as for me and my household, we will serve the LORD."
– *Joshua 24:14-15 NIV.*

Joshua challenged the Israelites to choose between two masters. Were they going to choose to serve God or serve idols? Joshua encourages the Israelites to make a personal commitment to serve the LORD. He boldly proclaims his allegiance by saying "As for me and my household, we will serve the LORD. Why does the bible say that we cannot serve two masters? Why does it say that we will love one and hate the other? Because when we are serving two masters, we are torn.

Are you torn between two masters? When we are in this situation of serving two masters, often we don't have peace in our lives, we might struggle to make the right decisions, we might not sleep well at night, and we can have animosity in our relationships. It's because we are sitting on the fence, so to speak. Talk about uncomfortable. Do you want to have peace in your life? Get off the fence and choose this day whom you serve, but as for me and my house, we WILL serve the LORD!

Memorize

"And if it seems evil not you to serve the LORD, choose you this day whom ye will serve… But as for me and my house, we will serve the LORD."

Joshua 24:15 KJV

Prayer

Lord, I love you and I love your word. Help me to fall more deeply in love with you and help me as I read today, to retain and understand what I am reading. I pray that you will speak to me through your word today and in this time of devotion.

Day 25

Read

Judges 7 to Judges 15

But the LORD said to Gideon, "There are still too many men. Take them down to the water and I will thin them out for you there. If I say, "This one shall go with you, he shall go, but if I say, 'This one shall not go with you, he shall not go. So, Gideon took the men down to the water. There the LORD told him, "Separate those who lap the water with their tongues as a dog laps, from those who kneel down to drink." Three hundred of them drank from cupped hands, lapping like dogs.

All the rest got down on their knees to drink. The LORD said to Gideon, "With the three hundred men that lapped I will save you and give the Midianites into your hands. Let all the others go home." – *Judges 7:4-7 NIV.*

In the Bible, God chose the "lappers" over the "kneelers". God feared that Gideon's large army would be able to take credit for the victory, therefore, he waddled Should be widdled it down to only three hundred men, ensuring that the credit could only be given to God. We know this because God said to Gideon, "The people with you are too many for me to give the Midianites into their hand, lest Israel boast over me, saying, "My own hand has saved me." God knew that with thirty-two thousand men, the Israelites could easily have assumed the win to be because they were strong and brave, but instead, God knocked the count down to three hundred men, so that they could not take any glory for the win themselves but know that they know that they know that the LORD saved them.

I love it when God proves Himself. It's scary being put in a situation where there is no way out unless God comes through, but Oh when He does. Our faith grows and we learn to trust Him more and more. This is why God did what He did with the Israelites, so that they knew that the only way they could win this battle, is if God came through, and He didn't disappoint.

Can you think of a time in your life, when you knew that you knew that you knew that God came through for you? Think about it, thank God for it, write it down, and hang on to it. It's times like these that help us get through any new challenges that come our way.

Memorize

"And if it seems evil not you to serve the LORD, Choose you this day whom ye will serve... But as for me and my house, we will serve the LORD."

Joshua 24:15 KJV

Prayer

Lord, I love you and I love your word. Help me to fall more deeply in love with you and help me as I read today, to retain and understand what I am reading. I pray that you will speak to me through your word today and in this time of devotion.

Day 26

Read

Judges 16 to 1 Samuel 2

But Ruth said, "Do not urge me to leave you or to return from following you. For where you go I will go, and where you lodge I will lodge. Your people shall be my people, and your God my God. Where you die, I will die, and there I will be buried. May the LORD do so to me and more also if anything but death parts me from you." *Ruth 1:15-17*

These are hard times that we are living in. Our country, which we have always felt safe and free in, leaves us having feelings of fear and uncertainty. I can imagine that is how Ruth must have felt when she was leaving her country to follow her mother-in-law, Naomi. She was leaving a country that she knew and felt safe, for a country of uncertainty.

A country that she must have heard stories of, from her husband. Stories of famine and loss. And she was choosing to leave the only thing she knew to go to this country of uncertainty. Why do you think she made this choice? I think it is because she fell in love with her mother-in-law's God. "Your people shall be my people and your God, my God", she had told her.

No matter what it took, Ruth was willing to leave everything she knew, all her comforts to be with the God that she knew Naomi had. I remember as a teenager hanging around with someone who was unlike anyone I had ever hung out with. This person loved the LORD and the God in Him was so attractive to me. I wanted to be around this person all the time and listen to him talk about Jesus. I attribute this person as being instrumental to me finding my way back to the LORD. Now, I want to be that person for other people.

Is there anyone in your life that when you spend time with them, you just know that they love the LORD? Do they challenge you in a good way? How about the other way around? Do you challenge anyone in a good way?

Memorize

"And if it seems evil not you to serve the LORD, Choose you this day whom ye will serve... But as for me and my house, we will serve the LORD."

Joshua 24:15 KJV

Prayer

Lord, I love you and I love your word. Help me to fall more deeply in love with you and help me as I read today, to retain and understand what I am reading. I pray that you will speak to me through your word today and in this time of devotion.

Day 27

Read

1 Samuel 3 to 1 Samuel 11

And the LORD came and stood, calling as at other times, "Samuel! Samuel!" And Samuel said, "Speak for your servant hears. Then the LORD said to Samuel, "Behold, I am about to do a thing in Israel at which the two ears of everyone who hears it will tingle. – *1 Samuel 3:10-11*

The Bible says that Samuel had not yet been introduced to the LORD, so this is the first time that Samuel had ever heard God's voice. Samuel's mother Hannah had made a deal with God, she said: "O LORD of hosts, if you will indeed look on the affliction of your servant and remember me and not forget your servant, but will give to your servant a son, then I will give him to the LORD all the days of his life and no razor shall touch his head."

God took the deal and gave Hannah a Son, and Hannah in return, gave Samuel to Eli, and the bible says that Samuel was ministering to the LORD under Eli. Imagine you are serving the LORD and the first thing he says to you is "Behold I am about to do a thing in Israel at which the two ears of everyone who hears it will tingle." What should Samuel do? What would you do? He's got to spill the beans to Eli, whose two sons were doing abominable things.

Sometimes God asks us to do things that are difficult, but if God asks, we may need to make difficult decisions and sometimes do difficult things.

Sometimes it may be telling someone that they are in sin, or sometimes it may be talking to someone about a direction they are taking that is not pleasing God, in other words, when God speaks, we need to have the same attitude that Samuel had and say, "Speak LORD, for your servant hears." If God is speaking to you, are you willing to listen?

Memorize

"And if it seems evil not you to serve the LORD, Choose you this day whom ye will serve... But as for me and my house, we will serve the LORD."

Joshua 24:15 KJV

Prayer

Lord, I love you and I love your word. Help me to fall more deeply in love with you and help me as I read today, to retain and understand what I am reading. I pray that you will speak to me through your word today and in this time of devotion.

Day 28

Spend today catching up on any days that you didn't get finished. It's important to enjoy God's word, and not to get overwhelmed if you fall behind, so today is a catch-up day, if you are caught up, it's a good day to spend looking back at what the LORD has spoken to you about, or even spend this hour in prayer. Today is the last day of your memory verse, so you can spend some time with your memory verse.

"And if it seems evil not you to serve the LORD, choose you this day whom ye will serve... But as for me and my house, we will serve the LORD."

Joshua 24:15 KJV

Day 29

Read

1 Samuel 12 to 1 Samuel 19

When they arrived, Samuel saw Eliab and thought, "Surely the LORD's anointed stands here before the LORD". But the LORD said to Samuel, "Do not consider his appearance or his height, for I have rejected him. The LORD does not look at the things people look at. People look at the outward appearance, but the LORD looks at the heart."– *1 Samuel 16:6-7 NIV.*

God doesn't do things the way man does them. The Bible says God's ways are higher than our ways (Isaiah 55:8-9). The world says to follow your heart, the word says to have the mind of Christ. 1 Corinthians 2:16. The world says to look after yourself first, the word says the first shall be last and last shall be first. The word says to reach for the top, the word says to consider others as more important than ourselves, the average Canadian spends $3000 per year on their appearance, but the word says beauty is fleeting.

This is why it is so important to set our affections on things above, not on things on this earth. *(Colossians 3:2),* and "Do not lean on your own understanding" *(Proverbs 3:5).* Let's start trying to do things a different way, let's try doing things, thinking about things, and consider things God's way, not man's way. Things might just start to make a whole lot more sense.

Memorize

But the LORD said unto Samuel, look not on his countenance, or on the height of his stature; because I have refused him: for the LORD seeth not as man seeth; for man looketh on the outward appearance, but the LORD looketh on the heart."

1 Samuel 16:7 KJV

Prayer

Lord, I love you and I love your word. Help me to fall more deeply in love with you and help me as I read today, to retain and understand what I am reading. I pray that you will speak to me through your word today and in this time of devotion.

Day 30

Read

1 Samuel 20 to 1 Samuel 29

And as soon as the boy had gone, David rose from beside the stone heap and fell on his face to the ground and bowed three times. And they kissed one another and wept with one another, David weeping the most. Then Jonathan said to David, "Go in peace, because we have sworn both of us in the name of the LORD saying, 'The LORD shall be between me and you, and between my offspring and your offspring, forever.'" And he rose and departed, and Jonathan went into the city. – *1 Samuel 20:41-42*

Relationships are a gift from God. Right from the beginning, God said that it was not good for man to be alone, so he gave Adam a helper, a companion. *Proverbs 18:24 says*, "One who has unreliable friends soon comes to ruin, but there is a friend who sticks closer than a brother.", *John 15:12 -13 says*, "My command is this: Love each other as I have loved you. Greater love has no one than this; to lay down one's life for one's friends, *1 Thessalonians 5:11 says*, "Therefore encourage one another and build one another up, just as you are doing."

In my lifetime, I have had healthy and unhealthy friendships. Healthy friendships build you up and help you to grow in your relationship with the LORD; Unhealthy friendships cause you to fall away and waste your time. This is also why it is so important to get involved in a local church.

We need community and we need to find people in our community who we can make ourselves accountable to, people to pray with and for, people to help us become better people. I have been in relationships that have drawn me away from a deeper relationship with the LORD and I have been in relationships that draw me closer to the LORD. I have spent time with people who drained my energy and I have spent time with people who have rejuvenated me.

What kinds of relationships do you have? If you are not spending time with people who are drawing you closer to the LORD, it's time to find new relationships.

Memorize

But the LORD said unto Samuel, look not on his countenance, or on the height of his stature; because I have refused him: for the LORD seeth not as man seeth; for man looketh on the outward appearance, but the LORD looketh on the heart."

1 Samuel 16:7 KJV

Prayer

Lord, I love you and I love your word. Help me to fall more deeply

in love with you and help me as I read today, to retain and understand what I am reading. I pray that you will speak to me through your word today and in this time of devotion.

Day 31

Read

1 Samuel 30 to 2 Samuel 9

And David said, "Is there still anyone left of the house of Saul, that I may show him kindness for Jonathan's sake?" – *2 Samuel 9:1*

We went on to read that there was still a son of Jonathan left, he was crippled in both his feet and his name was Mephibosheth. Because of Davids's relationship with Jonathan, Mephibosheth was given the honor of the son of a King. All the land that had belonged to Saul was restored to Mephibosheth and he ate at the Kings table every day. Mephibosheth asked, "What is your servant, that you should show regard for a dead dog such as I?"

It wasn't because of anything that Mephibosheth had done, in fact, it wasn't because of anything his father or his grandfather (the King before David) had done. It was because of David's love for Jonathan. This is the same for us. We are children of the King of Kings and the Lord of Lords. We are called the sons of God, not because of anything we have done, but because of what Jesus (the only Son of God) did for us. Like Mephibosheth, we didn't earn this position. David showed kindness (Mercy) to Jonathan's son. God showed kindness (Mercy) to us.

There are great applications that God wants us to get here.

1. Just as David kept his promise to Jonathan even though it cost him time, money, and energy, we recognize that the character of Christ is reflected in those who keep their word.

2. Just as Mephibosheth was saved by David's kindness and grace, and not because of anything that he himself did but because of what David did, we too are saved by God's kindness and grace and not because of anything we did, but because of what Christ did for us on the cross.

3. It had to be very humbling for Mephibosheth to accept "charity" from David when he was actually the grand-son of the previous King, but just as Mephibosheth accepted David's gift with humility, we too need to remember that when we come to God in humility, God will set a table before us in the presence of our enemies. God's word is filled with opportunities to find ways to apply the word to our lives.

Memorize

But the LORD said unto Samuel, look not on his countenance, or on the height of his stature; because I have refused him: for the LORD seeth not as man seeth; for man looketh on the outward appearance, but the LORD looketh on the heart."

1 Samuel 16:7 KJV

Prayer

Lord, I love you and I love your word. Help me to fall more deeply in love with you and help me as I read today, to retain and understand what I am reading. I pray that you would speak to me through your word today and in this time of devotions.

Day 32

Read

2 Samuel 10 to 2 Samuel 17

And Jehovah sent Nathan unto David. And he came unto him and said unto him. There were two men in one city, the one rich, and the other poor. The rich man had exceeded many flocks and herds, but the poor man had nothing, save one little ewe lamb, which he had bought and nourished up: and it grew up together with him, and with his children; it did eat of his own morsel, and drank of his own cup, and lay in his bosom, and was unto him as a daughter. And there came a traveler unto the rich man, and he spared to take of his own flock and of his own herd, to dress for the wayfaring man that was come unto him but took the poor man's lamb, and dressed it for the man that was come to him. – *2 Samuel 12:1-4 ASV*

David's sin broke God's heart but David didn't listen to the conviction of the Holy Spirit or to his own conscience. So, God had to send someone else to speak to David. God never lets sin go, he had to get a hold of David's heart and therefore God chose to send Nathan the profit to speak to David. He spoke in a way that David could hear. In God's mercy, he never let David go.

And David listened and repented, and David was called by God, a man after God's own heart. This wasn't because David never sinned, but because when he did, he was sorry and repented. It doesn't matter what we do, God loves us and is willing to forgive us. It's only up to us to "seek His face and pray and turn from our wicked ways."

If there is anything at all, big or small that should be given over to the Lord, don't waste time, repent. We need to take responsibility for our actions, seek God's forgiveness and the forgiveness of anyone we have wronged, and accept the consequences of our actions.

Memorize

But the LORD said unto Samuel, look not on his countenance, or on the height of his stature; because I have refused him: for the LORD seeth not as man seeth; for man looketh on the outward appearance, but the LORD looketh on the heart."

1 Samuel 16:7 KJV

Prayer

Lord, I love you and I love your word. Help me to fall more deeply in love with you and help me as I read today, to retain and understand what I am reading. I pray that you would speak to me through your word today and in this time of devotions.

Day 33

Read

2 Samuel 18 to 2 Samuel 24

David was conscience-stricken after he had counted the fighting men, and he said to the LORD, "I have sinned greatly in what I have done. Now, LORD, I beg you, take away the guilt of your servant. I have done a very foolish thing." Before David got up the next morning, the word of the LORD had come to Gad the prophet, David's seer: "Go and tell David, 'This is what the LORD says: I am giving you three options, choose one of them for me to carry out against you."

So, Gad went to David and said to him, "Shall there come on you three years of famine in your land? Or three months of fleeing from your enemies while they pursue you? Or three days of plague in your land? Now then, think it over and decide how I should answer the one who sent me." David said to Gad, "I am in deep distress. Let us fall into the hands of the LORD, for his mercy is great, but do not let me fall into human hands." – *2 Samuel 24:10-14 NIV*

David's decision to order a census went against the advice of Joab. Joab tried to persuade him not to take the census, which took almost 10 months to complete and resulted in numbering over a million citizens. The Bible says that God incited David to do this, right after the victory over the Philistines, the sin was probably related to a problem with pride and self-reliance. Needless to say, David knew that he had sinned, and when given the options, David knew that it was better to fall into the hands of God rather than into the hands of man. David understood the mercy of God, the faithfulness of God, and the goodness of God. God is a good God, and He loves you, and He is Sovereign.

When God allows things to happen to you, trust His goodness, trust His love for you, and trust that whatever happens is always for His glory and for your good.

Memorize

But the LORD said unto Samuel, look not on his countenance, or on the height of his stature; because I have refused him: for the LORD seeth not as man seeth; for man looketh on the outward appearance, but the LORD looketh on the heart."

1 Samuel 16:7 KJV

Prayer

Lord, I love you and I love your word. Help me to fall more deeply in love with you and help me as I read today, to retain and understand what I am reading. I pray that you would speak to me through your word today and in this time of devotions.

Day 34

Read

1 Kings 1 – 1 Kings 7

"And now, O LORD my God, you have made your servant king in place of David my father, although I am a little child. I do not know how to go out or come in. And your servant is in the midst of your people whom you have chosen, a great people, too many to be numbered or counted for multitude. Give your servant therefore an understanding mind to govern your people, that I may discern between good and evil, for who is able to govern this your great people?" *1 Kings 3:7-9 ESV*

We heard a sermon a few months ago about God preparing us to receive His blessing. Sometimes we are not ready for God's plan for our life. We may have sin in our lives, or a habit that might keep us from honoring God with the blessing He has planned for us. The one example our Pastor used was for those who are praying for a spouse, and the question was "Are you the person that the one you are asking the Lord for deserves?"

That stuck with me. Am I the person who can handle the blessing that God wants to give me? Since then, I have been praying less for what I want, and more that God will help me to be the person who deserves to have what He wants to give me. That is what Solomon did here 1 Kings 3. He didn't ask God for riches to rule his Kingdom, or for the favor of his people. He asked God to prepare Him for the task that God had placed on Him.

Take the time to think about what God might be preparing you for. What have you been asking the LORD for, and how can God help you to be the person who is ready to receive that request in your life?

Memorize

But the LORD said unto Samuel, look not on his countenance, or on the height of his stature; because I have refused him: for the LORD seeth not as man seeth; for man looketh on the outward appearance, but the LORD looketh on the heart."

1 Samuel 16:7 KJV

Prayer

Lord, I love you and I love your word. Help me to fall more deeply in love with you and help me as I read today, to retain and understand what I am reading. I pray that you would speak to me through your word today and in this time of devotions.

Day 35

Spend today catching up on any days that you didn't get finished. It's important to enjoy God's word, and not to get overwhelmed if you fall behind, so today is a catch-up day, OR, if you are caught up, it's a good day to spend looking back at what the Lord has spoken to you about, or even spend this hour in prayer. Today is the last day of your memory verse, so you can spend some time with your memory verse.

But the LORD said unto Samuel, look not on his countenance, or on the height of his stature; because I have refused him: for the LORD seeth not as man seeth; for man looketh on the outward appearance, but the LORD looketh on the heart."

1 Samuel 16:7 KJV

Day 36

Read

1 Kings 8 to 1 Kings 14

Jeroboam and all the assembly of Israel came and said to Rehoboam, "Your father made our yoke heavy. Now therefore lighten the hard service of your father and his heavy yoke on us, and we will serve you." He said to them, "Go away, for three days, then come again to me." So, the people went away. – *1 Kings 12:3-5*

And the King answered the people harshly, and forsaking the counsel that the old men had given him, he spoke to them according to the counsel of the young men, saying, "My father made your yoke heavy, but I will add to your yoke. My father disciplined you with whips, but I will discipline you with scorpions." – *1 Kings 12:13-14*

Whenever I read this passage, it makes me think of a child in kindergarten. Almost like he was too young to rule. He had to consult his friends whom he grew up with instead of the counsel of those His father used. Rehoboam started off his reign as a very prideful, very arrogant King. He had such a high opinion of himself. Jeroboam was so conceited and proud in his narcissistic persona, that he felt himself above being answerable to anyone but himself. I can almost hear, "nananananana" as he chose to please himself without considering anyone or anything else.

The Bible says "God opposes the proud, but gives grace to the humble." *(James 4:6-8).* Why? Because essentially, in refusing to trust God and provide what we need ourselves is an act of pride and is attempting to be the God of our own lives.

Memorize

"O LORD God of Israel, there is no God like you in heaven above or on earth beneath, keeping covenant and showing steadfast love to your servants who walk before you with all their heart."

1 Kings 8:23

Prayer

Lord, I love you and I love your word. Help me to fall more deeply in love with you and help me as I read today, to retain and understand what I am reading. I pray that you would speak to me through your word today and in this time of devotions.

Day 37

Read

1 Kings 15 to 1 Kings 21

After a long time, in the third year, the word of the LORD came to Elijah: "Go and present yourself to Ahab, and I will send rain on the land." So, Elijah went to present himself to Ahab. Now the famine was severe in Samaria and Ahab had summoned Obadiah, his palace administrator. (Obadiah was a devout believer in the LORD.

While Jezebel was killing off the LORD's prophets, Obadiah had taken a hundred prophets and hidden them in two caves, fifty in each, and had supplied them with food and water.) – *1 Kings 18:1-4 NIV*

Okay so just a little fun fact, this Obadiah is the same Obadiah who wrote the book of Obadiah. What a man of God. 1 Kings calls him a man who feared the LORD greatly and it tells how he hid the prophets of the LORD. In the book of Obadiah, he reminds us to place ourselves under God's authority. He announces Edom's downfall. Obadiah is such a small book, one that many people have never read and yet it is a book written by a great prophet. Obadiah may not be remembered by a whole lot of people, but he did great things for the LORD. He spent his own wealth feeding and supporting the 100 prophets he had hidden from Jezebel, in fact, eventually, Obadiah had to borrow money from Ahab's son to continue supporting them.

Obadiah definitely had his priorities right. He made a choice to hide 100 prophets of the LORD from the evil Jezebel and spent all his wealth to do it. Is there something you have given up or should be giving up to do something that God is asking you to do? God is worth it.

Memorize

"O LORD God of Israel, there is no God like you in heaven above or on earth beneath, keeping covenant and showing steadfast love to your servants who walk before you with all their heart."

1 Kings 8:23

Prayer

Lord, I love you and I love your word. Help me to fall more deeply in love with you and help me as I read today, to retain and understand what I am reading. I pray that you would speak to me through your word today and in this time of devotions.

Day 38

Read

1 Kings 22 to 2 Kings 7

When they had crossed, Elijah said to Elisha, "Ask what I shall do for you before I am taken from you." And Elisha said, "Please let there be a double portion of your spirit on me." And he said, "You have asked a hard thing; yet, if you see me as I am being taken from you, it shall be so for you, but if you do not see me, it shall not be so." And as they still went on and talked, behold, chariots of fire and horses of fire separated the two of them. And Elijah went up by a whirlwind into heaven. And Elisha saw it and he cried, "My father, my father! The chariots of Israel and its horsemen!" And he saw him no more. – *2 Kings 2:9-12 ESV*

The entire time, Elisha was following Elijah; He knew that Elijah was going to be taken from him, but Elisha was focused on fulfilling God's plan for his life. He was to fill Elijah's sandals, so to speak, and he wanted to ensure that he was ready. Elijah kept telling him, stay here, I have to go to Bethel (which means house of God), stay here, I have to go to Jericho (which means place of fragrance), stay here, I have to go to the Jordan (which represents Freedom from oppression, breakthrough and deliverance). Each time, Elisha refused to be left out of whatever it was that God had for him.

He was focused. When Elijah asked him, "What do you want from me", all Elisha wanted was to be worthy to put on his mantle, so he asked for a double portion of his spirit. Elijah told him that only if he saw him leaving, would he receive this. There was so much that could have distracted Elisha, but Elisha was not to be distracted, not by the chariots of fire and not by the horses of fire. Things that typically would have distracted even the most focused of people, but not Elisha, he saw Elijah going up in the whirlwind and therefore was given a double portion of his spirit.

What distracts you from God's plan in your life? Take the time to give Him your distractions and ask Him to help you focus on His plan for your life.

Memorize

"O LORD God of Israel, there is no God like you in heaven above or on earth beneath, keeping covenant and showing steadfast love to your servants who walk before you with all their heart."

1 Kings 8:23

Prayer

Lord, I love you and I love your word. Help me to fall more deeply in love with you and help me as I read today, to retain and understand what I am reading. I pray that you would speak to me through your word today and in this time of devotions.

Day 39

Read

2 Kings 8 to 2 Kings 15

In the seventh year of Jehu, Jehoash began to reign, and he reigned forty years in Jerusalem. His mother's name was Zibiah of Beersheba. And Jehoash did what was right in the eyes of the LORD all his days because Jehoiada the priest instructed him. Nevertheless, the high places were not taken away; the people continued to sacrifice and make offerings on (should be on) the high places. – *2 Kings 12:1-3 ESV*

Jehoash did what was right in the eyes of the LORD all the days in which Jehoiada the priest instructed him. The implication here is that when Jehoiada died, Jehoash turned away from right practices. 2 Chronicles 24 tells us that Jehoash turned to idolatry when the Priest Jehoiada died. After Jehoiada died, Jehoash had ungodly advisors who turned his heart away from serving God.

Jehoash's life is a great testament as to why we need God-fearing people in our lives and why Titus 2 teaches that older women are to be reverent in the way they live, not slanderers and not addicted to much wine, but to teach what is good so that they can teach younger women to love their husbands and children, be self-controlled, be pure, be busy at home, kind, and to teach them to be subject to their own husbands. Jehoash is a great example of why young men and women should find mentors in older men and women. They should find someone who is a godly influence, who is kind, and thoughtful, a good husband or wife, a good mother or father, someone who is an example of Christ and knows the word of God.

Are you either a mentor or have a mentor in your life? If you are younger, find a godly older person who can speak into your life and help you to be the person that God created you to be. If you are older, find a younger person who you can pour into their lives and help them to make a difference for the Kingdom of God.

Memorize

"O LORD God of Israel, there is no God like you in heaven above or on earth beneath, keeping covenant and showing steadfast love to your servants who walk before you with all their heart."

1 Kings 8:23

Prayer

Lord, I love you and I love your word. Help me to fall more deeply in love with you and help me as I read today, to retain and understand what I am reading. I pray that you would speak to me through your word today and in this time of devotions.

Day 40

Read

2 Kings 16 to 2 Kings 23

Tell the King of Judah, who sent you to inquire of the LORD, "This is what the LORD, the God of Israel says concerning the words you heard: Because your heart was responsive and you humbled yourself before the LORD when you heard what I have spoken against this place and its people – that they would become a curse and be laid waste – and because you tore your robes and wept in my presence, I also have heard you, declares the LORD.

Therefore, I will gather you to your ancestors, and you will be buried in peace. Your eyes will not see all the disaster I am going to bring to this place." So, they took her answer back to the king. *2 Kings 22:18-20 NIV*

Josiah sent the secretary to the house of the LORD to Hilkiah the high priest, and Hilkiah told the secretary that he found a book of the law in the house of the LORD. Shaphan, the secretary, read it and told Josiah what it said. Josiah was devastated. He tore his clothes (which was a sign of deep sorrow and remorse). Joshiah was a very young King; he was only 8 years old when he first started his reign; yet he tore down the high places and was a king who did what was right in the eyes of the LORD.

Though he had never even heard of the book of the law, upon hearing what it says, Josiah tore his clothes and said to Shaphan and others to go and inquire of the LORD, not just for himself, but for the people and for all Judah concerning the words of this book that has been found. Josiah said, "For great is the wrath of the LORD that is kindled against us, because our fathers have not obeyed the words of this book, to do according to all that is written concerning us." *2 Kings 22:13.*

It wasn't even for his disobedience, but for what their fathers had not obeyed. God is always looking for that heart that follows after him. He chose to bring disaster to the people after Josiah's reign. God loves a repentant heart.

We often blame our upbringing for the way we turned out. Our parents didn't do their job, or we came from a broken home. There are a thousand reasons we can blame our upbringing for the mess we became, but we are responsible for how we respond to the hurts of our past. Josiah didn't blame his ancestors, he actually repented on behalf of them. It's time to stop looking for excuses for why we are messed up, and run to the LORD with our hearts, tear our robes (so to speak), and make a difference instead of making excuses.

Memorize

"O LORD God of Israel, there is no God like you in heaven above or on earth beneath, keeping covenant and showing steadfast love to your servants who walk before you with all their heart."

1 Kings 8:23

Prayer

Lord, I love you and I love your word. Help me to fall more deeply in love with you and help me as I read today, to retain and understand what I am reading. I pray that you would speak to me through your word today and in this time of devotions.

Day 41

Read

2 Kings 24 to 1 Chronicles 7

And in the ninth year of his reign, in the tenth month, on the tenth day of the month, Nebuchadnezzar, king of Babylon came with all his army against Jerusalem and laid siege to it. And they built siegeworks all around it. – *2 Kings 25: 1 ESV*

God gave the Israelites plenty of warning. He told them that he was going to send them into captivity. He informed Hezekiah that this was going to happen. God allowed the Babylonians to destroy Jerusalem and strip the Temple of almost everything that mattered. After years of disobedience, God allowed Nebuchadnezzar to take His people into captivity for several decades. Why? Because God cares more about His people than what His people are going through. In fact, He ordained this. He caused this to happen so that His people would repent and return to Him. They were far from God, and they had years of disobeying Him, and He was willing to lead them into captivity in order to eventually see them free.

We often hear people ask "Why does God allow bad things to happen?" I have had my fair share of bad things happen to me, but every time, (Although I never see this until I'm through it) it has been for God's glory and for my good." The bible says "And we know that to them that love God all things work together for good, even to them that are called according to His purpose." *(Romans 8:28 ASV)* I see God working in my life through all the trials I have gone through and in hindsight, I wouldn't want it any other way because He loves me and everything He allows, He allows for a purpose. What have you gone through, or are you going through that you haven't thanked the LORD for? Go to Him and thank Him that what you are allowing is for your good and for His glory.

Memorize

"O LORD God of Israel, there is no God like you in heaven above or on earth beneath, keeping covenant and showing steadfast love to your servants who walk before you with all their heart."

1 Kings 8:23

Prayer

Lord, I love you and I love your word. Help me to fall more deeply in love with you and help me as I read today, to retain and understand what I am reading. I pray that you would speak to me through your word today and in this time of devotions.

Day 42

Spend today catching up on any days that you didn't get finished. It's important to enjoy God's word, and not to get overwhelmed if you fall behind, so today is a catch-up day, OR, if you are caught up, it's a good day to spend looking back at what the Lord has spoken to you about, or even spend this hour in prayer. Today is the last day of your memory verse, so you can spend some time with your memory verse.

"O LORD God of Israel, there is no God like you in heaven above or on earth beneath, keeping covenant and showing steadfast love to your servants who walk before you with all their heart."

1 Kings 8:23

Day 43

Read

1 Chronicles 8 to 1 Chronicles 16

David consulted with the captains of thousands and of hundreds, even with every leader. And David said unto all the assembly of Israel, if it seems good unto you and if it be of Jehovah our God, let us send abroad unto our brethren that are left in all the land of Israel, with whom the priests and Levites are in the cities that have suburbs, that they may gather themselves unto us and let us bring again the ark of our God to us, for we sought not unto it in the days of Saul.

… And they carried the ark of God upon a new cart, and brought it out of the house of Abinadab, the Uzza and Ahio drove the cart. And David and all Israel played before God with all their might, with songs and with harps and with psalteries, and with timbrels, and with cymbals, and with trumpets. And when they came unto the threshing floor of Chidon, Uzza put forth his hand to hold off the ark, for the oxen stumbled. And the anger of Jehovah was kindled against Uzza, and he smote him because he put forth his hand to the ark, and there he died before God. – *1 Chronicles 13: 1-3 & 7-10 ASV*

As the ark of God was being transported, the oxen stumbled and Uzza took hold of the ark God's anger burned toward Uzza and struck him and he died. Seems extreme, doesn't it? God had given

Moses and Aaron specific instructions when he told them how to move the Ark of the Covenant. First of all, as we read in Numbers 4:15 says "And when Aaron and his sons have finished covering the sanctuary and all the furnishings of the sanctuary, as the camp sets out, after that the sons of Kohath shall come to carry these, but they must not touch the holy things, lest they die."

Only the sons of Kohath were to carry the holy things and Second, Exodus *25: 12-15* tells us that they were not to touch it, but were to put it on a pole, with gold rings, and carry it on their shoulders. Uzza was just trying to save the ark, however, that was in direct violation of God's law, as we read above. Obeying God's law was a means of preserving God's holiness and reminding His people not to draw near to God without appropriate preparation but with reverence and fear.

We might have the best of intentions in the things we do, and we might even do them to glorify the LORD, but we still might displease God if we are doing these things on our own strength instead of in His strength. Are you keeping busy doing Kingdom work? Are you doing it to please the LORD? Or are you doing it to look good? Most of my Christian walk was doing things to look like Super Christians, and I ended up burning out because I was doing it in my own strength. Make sure that what you are doing (even for the LORD), you are doing it to bring Glory to the LORD, not make yourself look good.

Memorize

And he sought God in the days of Zechariah, who had understanding in the visions of God: and as long as he sought the LORD, God made him to prosper.

2 Chronicles 26:5 KJV

Prayer

Lord, I love you and I love your word. Help me to fall more deeply in love with you and help me as I read today, to retain and understand what I am reading. I pray that you would speak to me through your word today and in this time of devotions.

Day 44

Read

1 Chronicles 17 to 1 Chronicles 24

Then King David went in and sat before the LORD and said, "Who am I, O LORD God, and what is my house, that you have brought me thus far? And this was a small thing in your eyes, O God. You have also spoken of your servant's house for a great while to come, and have shown me future generation, O LORD God! And what more can David say to you for honoring your servant? For you know your servant. For your servant's sake, O LORD, and according to your own heart, you have done all this greatness, in making known all these great things. There is none like you, O LORD, and there is no God besides you, according to all that we have heard with our ears." *1 Chronicles 17:16-20*

The Bible calls David a man after God's own heart. I don't think it is because of all the great things David did, I think it is because David was a man of humility. When he had the opportunity (twice) to kill Saul, he refused to put his hand toward God's anointed, and when the Ark of the Covenant was brought home, he allowed himself to be despised in the eyes of his wife Michal in order to show his obsession with the LORD, and when God wanted to bless David, his answer to the LORD was, "Who am I O LORD and what is my house. We know who he was, and what his house was, but David remained humble before the LORD because when he received this wonderful gift, it didn't make him think of himself as any greater, instead in David's eyes, it made God greater.

Our dreams for our lives may not match God's vision for ourselves. We need to be open to God's vision for our lives. We very well may miss out on a greater purpose if we choose our way instead of God's way. *Proverbs 16:9* says "The heart of man plans his way but the LORD establishes his steps" What are some areas in your life where you need to surrender your ideals and give God all your plans, allowing Him to do His work in your life?

Memorize

And he sought God in the days of Zechariah, who had understanding in the visions of God: and as long as he sought the LORD, God made him to prosper.

2 Chronicles 26:5 KJV

Prayer

Lord, I love you and I love your word. Help me to fall more deeply in love with you and help me as I read today, to retain and understand what I am reading. I pray that you would speak to me through your word today and in this time of devotions.

Day 45

Read

1 Chronicles 25 to 2 Chronicles 6

All these were the sons of Heman the king's seer, according to the promise of God to exult him, for God had given Heman fourteen sons and three daughters. They were all under the direction of their father in the music in the house of the LORD with cymbals, harps, and lyres for the service of the house of God. Asaph, Jeduthun, and Heman were under the order of the king. The number of them along with their brothers, who were trained in singing to the LORD, all who were skillful, was 288. *1 Chronicles 25:5-7*

David chose three men to lead the musical worship at the Temple in Jerusalem after it was completed. Why? David recognized the connection between the security of His Kingdom and the Ministry of Worship. Worship was the instrument that God used to lead many battles. Gideon, who had only 300 men to defeat the Midianites, did so with jars and trumpets; the Israelites defeated Jericho by walking around the walls and blowing their trumpets, and when the Ark was brought back to the camp, there was singing and dancing. God used worship to defeat armies.

David recognized that in building the House of the LORD, worship was an important part. I believe that the enemy cringes during our worship time, I always feel ushered into the presence of the LORD during our worship time. But music is only one part of worship, I believe we can look around at God's creation and worship, we can look at a newborn baby and worship.

Worship is an important means that God uses in battle. John Piper puts it well when he states that worship was designed to "put the supreme worth of God on display". (Desiring God). Worship isn't just what we do on Sunday mornings before and after the sermon, it is being reverent in the Presence of the LORD, remembering His Greatness, and being in awe of His Holiness. In essence, it is recognizing the awesomeness of God. Have you made worship a part of your day today? It's never too late.

Memorize

And he sought God in the days of Zechariah, who had understanding in the visions of God: and as long as he sought the LORD, God made him to prosper.

2 Chronicles 26:5 KJV

Prayer

Lord, I love you and I love your word. Help me to fall more deeply in love with you and help me as I read today, to retain and understand what I am reading. I pray that you would speak to me through your word today and in this time of devotions.

Day 46

Read

2 Chronicles 7 to 2 Chronicles 18

Ahab king of Israel said unto Jehoshaphat king of Judah, "Wilt thou go with me to Ramoth-Gilead?" And he answered him, "I am as thou art, and my people as thy people and we will be with thee in the war." And Jehoshaphat said unto the king of Israel, "Enquire I pray thee at the word of the LORD today." Therefore, the king of Israel gathered together of prophets four hundred men and said unto them, "Shall we go to Ramoth-Gilead to battle or shall I forbear?" And they said, "Go up, for God will deliver it into the king's hand." But Jehoshaphat said, "Is there not here a prophet of the LORD besides, that we may enquire of him?" *2 Chronicles 18:3-6 KJV*

Jehoshaphat wouldn't go until he knew that he heard from the LORD. He heard from 400 prophets, but he knew that something wasn't right. He discerned that God hadn't spoken to these men, and he asked, "Is there not here another prophet of the LORD of whom we may inquire?" It's so easy for us when we want to make choices to listen to people who tell us what we want to hear. It's easier to hear the positive than the negative. It is so important to have people in our lives who tell us what we need to hear, not just what we want to hear. In our last church, I had many "friends". They all told me what I wanted to hear. When everything fell apart in my life, most of my "friends" fell away. Since attending my church, (Crossroads Bible Church), I have people who speak into my life because they care about my relationship with the LORD more than they care about my relationship with them.

Do you have those people in your life? Tell them how much they mean to you. If you don't have those people in your life, ask the LORD to help you find them.

Memorize

And he sought God in the days of Zechariah, who had understanding in the visions of God: and as long as he sought the LORD, God made him to prosper.

2 Chronicles 26:5 KJV

Prayer

Lord, I love you and I love your word. Help me to fall more deeply in love with you and help me as I read today, to retain and understand what I am reading. I pray that you would speak to me through your word today and in this time of devotions.

Day 47

Read

2 Chronicles 19 to 2 Chronicles 31

But when he was strong, his heart was lifted up to his destruction: for he transgressed against the LORD his God and went into the temple of the LORD to burn incense upon the altar of incense. And Azariah the priest went in after him and with him, fourscore priests of the LORD that were valiant men: And they withstood Uzziah the King and said unto him, It appertaineth not unto thee, Uzziah, to burn incense unto the LORD, but o the priests the sons of Aaron, that are consecrated to burn incense: go out of the sanctuary; for thou has trespassed; neither shall it be for thine honor from the Lord God. Then Uzziah was worth and had a censer in his hand to burn incense: and while he was wroth with the priests, the leprosy even rose up in his forehead before the priests in the house of the LORD, from beside the incense altar.

And Azariah the chief priest, and all the priests, looked upon him, and behold, he was leprous in his forehead and they thrust him out from thence; yea, himself hasted also to go out, because the LORD had smitten him. And Uzziah the king was a leper unto the day of his death, and dwelt in several houses, being a leper; for he was cut off from the house of the LORD; and Jothan his son was over the king's house, judging the people of the land. *2 Chronicles 26: 16-21 KJV.*

King Uzziah, the bible says did what was right in the eyes of the LORD, in fact, in this same chapter in verses 4 and 5, it says "He did what was right in the eyes of the LORD according to all that his father had done. He set himself to seek God in the days of Zechariah, who instructed him in the fear of God, and as long as he sought the LORD, God made him prosper. Yet because of pride, because he grew strong, and did great things, he became prideful. Do you see a pattern here? Scripture tells us the "Pride cometh before a fall and a haughty spirit before destruction" *Proverbs 16:18.*

I've seen great people fall because they took the glory for what the LORD had done through them. I pray all the time, "God, help me to give you the glory for all that you have done, God, keep me humble, God, help me to put others first. As much as I pray this, I still fail often. I care about what others think about me too often instead of caring about others first.

Do you struggle with pride? Ask the LORD to help you in the areas you struggle with.

Memorize

And he sought God in the days of Zechariah, who had understanding in the visions of God: and as long as he sought the LORD, God made him to prosper.

2 Chronicles 26:5 KJV

Prayer

Lord, I love you and I love your word. Help me to fall more deeply in love with you and help me as I read today, to retain and understand what I am reading. I pray that you would speak to me through your word today and in this time of devotions.

Day 48

Read

2 Chronicles 32 to Ezra 3

And when the builders laid the foundation of the temple of the LORD, they set the priests in their apparel with trumpets, and the Levites, the sons of Asaph, with cymbals, to praise the LORD, after the ordinance of David King of Israel. And they sang together by course in praising and giving thanks unto the LORD; because He is good, for His mercy endureth forever toward Israel. And all the people shouted with a great shout when they praised the LORD because the foundation of the house of the LORD was laid.

But many of the priests and Levites and chief of fathers who were ancient men that had seen the first house, when the foundation of this house laid before their eyes, wept with a loud voice; and many shouted aloud for joy: So that the people could not discern the noise of the shout of joy from the noise of the weeping of the people: for the people shouted with a loud shout, and the noise was heard afar off. *Ezra 3: 10-13 KJV*

The first thing that the former exiles did was to rebuild the temple and thereby set up the altar of God in order to sacrifice burnt offerings to the LORD. These verses capture the essence of worship. It speaks to the deep longing of the Israelites to reconnect with God.

In this chapter, you see the people all coming together to worship and give thanks and proclaim the goodness of God, even during hardship and trials. It is so important for us to take the time to count our blessings but also, as the song says, 'When darkness closes in LORD, still I will say "Blessed be the Name of the LORD."'

Just as the people came together to give thanks for God's goodness in their lives even in the midst of trials, so we should take the time to count our blessings and honor God in all our circumstances.

Memorize

And he sought God in the days of Zechariah, who had understanding in the visions of God: and as long as he sought the LORD, God made him to prosper.

2 Chronicles 26:5 KJV

Prayer

Lord, I love you and I love your word. Help me to fall more deeply in love with you and help me as I read today, to retain and understand what I am reading. I pray that you will speak to me through your word today and in this time of devotion.

Day 49

Spend today catching up on any days that you didn't get finished. It's important to enjoy God's word, and not to get overwhelmed if you fall behind, so today is a catch-up day, OR, if you are caught up, it's a good day to spend looking back at what the Lord has spoken to you about, or even spend this hour in prayer. Today is the last day of your memory verse, so you can spend some time with your memory verse.

And he sought God in the days of Zechariah, who had understanding in the visions of God: and as long as he sought the LORD, God made him to prosper.

2 Chronicles 26:5 KJV

Day 50

Read

Ezra 4 to Ezra 10

Blessed be the LORD God of our fathers, which hath put such a thing as this in the king's heart, to beautify the house of the LORD which is in Jerusalem: And hath extended mercy unto me before the king and his counselors and before all the king's mighty princes. And I was strengthened as the hand of the LORD my God was upon me, and I gathered together out of Israel chief men to go up with me. *Ezra 7: 27-28 KJV*

The people of God were captured and sent to a foreign land with foreign gods and yet the influence they had over these lands was amazing. Cyrus, Darius, and Artaxerxes all assisted in the rebuilding of the temple. Not by physically doing the labour, but by writing letters allowing the rebuilding and even supplying provisions. I know we live in scary times with a government that is "anti-Christ", but God is still on His throne and He is writing our story and He loves us, and He is in control. We are to fear not. But watch and see what the LORD can do, is doing, and will do.

Talk to God about your fears, and allow him to show you, His goodness.

Memorize

"For I know that my redeemer liveth, and that He shall stand at the latter day upon the earth."

Job 19:25 KJV

Prayer

Lord, I love you and I love your word. Help me to fall more deeply in love with you and help me as I read today, to retain and understand what I am reading. I pray that you will speak to me through your word today and in this time of devotion.

Day 51

Read

Nehemiah 1 to Nehemiah 9

And said, I beseech thee, O LORD God of heaven, the great and terrible God that keepeth covenant and mercy for them that love him and observe his commandments. Let thine ear now be attentive and thine eyes open, that thou mayest hear the prayer of thy servant, which I pray before thee now, day and night, for the children of Israel thy servants and confess the sins of the children of Israel, which we have sinned against thee. Both I and my father's house have sinned. We have dealt very corruptly against thee, and have not kept the commandments, nor the statutes, nor the judgments, which thou commandesdst thy servant Moses.

Remember, I beseech thee, the word that thou commandest thy servant Moses, saying, 'If ye transgress, I will scatter you abroad among the nations: But if ye turn unto me, and keep my commandments and do them, though there were of you cast out unto the uttermost part of the heaven, yet will I gather them from thence, and will bring them unto the place that I have chosen to set my name there.

Now these are they servants and thy people, whom thou hast redeemed by thy great power, and by thy strong hand. O LORD, I beseech thee, let now thine ear be attentive to the prayer of thy servant, and to the prayer of thy servant, and to the prayer of thy servants, who desire to fear thy name: and prosper, I pray thee, thy servant this day, and grant him mercy in the sight of this man. For I was the king's cupbearer. - *Nehemiah 1:5-11 KJV*

This was Nehemiah's prayer after he heard that the remnant in the province who had survived the exile was in great trouble and shame and that the wall of Jerusalem was broken down and its gates were destroyed by fire. Nehemiah gets this really bad news and he spends time repenting for what they had done to bring about this disaster. But God had given them a way out, hadn't he? "If my people who are called by my name, will humble themselves and pray and seek my face and turn from their wicked ways, then I will hear from heaven and heal their land. *Jeremiah 29:11.*

So, Nehemiah was saying, we sinned, we are sorry, we will change, please heal our land. Nehemiah recognized that Prayer is essential.

Take some time to look at your life to see if there is anything you need to confess to the LORD. As a believer, you need to identify your needs and seek God in prayer. God is able and willing to answer prayer.

Memorize

"For I know that my redeemer liveth, and that He shall stand at the latter day upon the earth."

Job 19:25 KJV

Prayer

Lord, I love you and I love your word. Help me to fall more deeply in love with you and help me as I read today, to retain and understand what I am reading. I pray that you will speak to me through your word today and in this time of devotion.

Day 52

Read

Nehemiah 10 to Esther 10

Then Mordecai told them to reply to Esther, "Do not think to yourself that in the king's palace, you will escape any more than all the other Jews. For if you keep silent at this time, relief and deliverance will rise for the Jews from another place, but you and your father's house will perish. And who knows whether you have not come to the kingdom for such a time as this?"

Then Esther told them to reply to Mordecai, "Go, gather all the Jews to be found in Susa, and hold a fast on my behalf, and do not eat or drink for three days, night or day. I and my young women will also be as fast as you are. Then I will go to the king, though it is against the law, and if I perish, I perish. *Esther 4:13-16*

One of my favorite books of the Bible is the Book of Esther. She was so brave and Mordecai was a godly man so full of wisdom. He was such a good stepfather type to Esther. She was sent to the palace, where Mordecai watched over her daily from the king's gate. He loved Esther so much, that it must have been hard for him to ask her to go to the king on behalf of their people, yet, he knew it was the right thing to do. "Who knows whether you have not come to the kingdom for such a time as this?" If we had this attitude "that we are in this situation for such a time as this", then so many things that happen in our lives, might make more sense.

God has written our story, He loves us, and He does everything for His Glory and for our good. So, whatever we are going through is probably "for such a time as this". I know it is hard to go through various trials, but Esther was brave… Her answer was, I will do this thing, though it is against the law, and if I perish, I perish. WOW!

As we read this passage, we see how Esther was willing to possibly give up her life to save her people, and to make a difference. And we also see how faithful God was when she did. My prayer is that as I go through various trials in my life, I do so with the same attitude as Esther did. I recognize that I am in this trial for such a time as this, and if I perish, I perish. How do you feel when you go through trials in your life? Think about it as you ponder God's will for your life, and what is he asking you to do.

Memorize

"For, I know that my redeemer liveth, and that He shall stand at the latter day upon the earth."

Job 19:25 KJV

Prayer

Lord, I love you and I love your word. Help me to fall more deeply

in love with you and help me as I read today, to retain and understand what I am reading. I pray that you will speak to me through your word today and in this time of devotion.

Day 53

Read

Job 1 to Job 12

And the LORD said to Satan, "From where have you come? "Satan answered the LORD and said, "From going to and from on the earth, and from walking up and down on it." And the LORD said to Satan, "Have you considered my servant Job, that there is none like him on the earth, a blameless and upright man, who fears God and turns away from evil? He still holds fast to his integrity, although you incited me against him to destroy him without reason." *Job 2:2-3*

The Bible says, "Consider it pure joy, my brothers and sisters, whenever you face trials of many kinds because you know that the testing of your faith produces perseverance. Let perseverance finish its work so that you may be mature and complete, not lacking anything. James 1:2-4 God doesn't allow things in our lives for fun. Nothing we go through is trivial. He has a purpose and that purpose is so that we may be mature and complete, lacking in nothing. He knows what is good for us, and everything done in our lives is done for His Glory and for our good, therefore, whatever we are going through, (and we are all going through something), let's consider it pure joy. Job had everything taken away from him, but as you continue to read this book, you will see that everything truly did work out for God's Glory and for his good.

When Job was suffering all that loss, he chose not to "curse God and die" as his wife told him to do. What is your attitude when suffering through trials?

Memorize

"For I know that my redeemer liveth, and that He shall stand at the latter day upon the earth."

Job 19:25 KJV

Prayer

Lord, I love you and I love your word. Help me to fall more deeply in love with you and help me as I read today, to retain and understand what I am reading. I pray that you would speak to me through your word today and in this time of devotions.

Day 54

Read
Job 13 to Job 27

"As God lives, who has taken away my right, and the Almighty, who has made my soul bitter, as long as my breath is in me, and the spirit of God is in my nostrils, my lips will not speak falsehood, and my tongue will not utter deceit. Far be it from me to say that you are right; till I die I will not put away my integrity from me. I hold fast to my righteousness and will not let it go; my heart does not reproach me for any of my days. - *Job 27:2-6*

This chapter began with Job declaring his integrity, despite all the suffering he was facing. He wanted to hold onto his righteousness at any cost and not let it go. Imagine how it must have felt for Job. He knew that God was allowing all these trials. And yet, he would not let go of his integrity. He was in pain, yet, he would not let go of his integrity. He lost his family, yet, he would not let go of his integrity.

He lost his livelihood, yet, he would not let go of his integrity. His wife was angry at him and told him to curse God and die, yet, he would not let go of his integrity. I am not belittling any of your trials, any of your loss, any of your pain, but God knows what you are going through and He loves you, and He is in control and on His throne and He is allowing this, (for such a time as this) for His Glory and for your good.

There is definitely a theme in the bible for our lives. We will go through trials, God loves us, God is Sovereign and nothing we go through is trivial. If you are able, thank Him for whatever you are going through, and ask him to help you not let go of his integrity.

Memorize

"For I know that my redeemer liveth, and that He shall stand at the latter day upon the earth."

Job 19:25 KJV

Prayer

Lord, I love you and I love your word. Help me to fall more deeply in love with you and help me as I read today, to retain and understand what I am reading. I pray that you would speak to me through your word today and in this time of devotions.

Day 55

Read

Job 28 to Job 40

Then the LORD answered Job out of the whirlwind and said: Who is this that darkens counsel by words without knowledge? Dress for action like a man; I will question you and you make it known to me. Where were you when I laid the foundation of the earth? Tell me, if you understand. Who determined its measurements – surely you know! Or who stretched the line upon it? On what were its bases sunk, or who laid its cornerstone, when the morning stars sang together, and all the sons of God shouted for joy? Or who shut in the sea with doors when it burst out from the womb, when I made clouds its garment and thick darkness its swaddling band, and prescribed limits for it and set bars and doors, and said, 'Thus far you shall come, and no farther, and here shall your proud waves be stayed. *Job 38:1-11*

Seriously? Who even knew that the stars sang in the morning, who knew that the clouds have their own garments? Who knew that God commanded the waves to go so far and no further? No wonder He was able to part the Red Sea so His people could walk across on dry ground. No wonder when Elijah prayed, God could stop the rain from falling for a few years. No wonder when the Israelites were hungry, manna from heaven showed up every morning. No wonder a large fish was able to swallow up Jonah and spit him out again alive. No wonder a donkey found his voice and was able to speak to Balaam and save his life. And no wonder when the government told us to close our doors and we chose to obey God rather than man, he grew our congregation so that we had to knock out walls and buy new chairs. He is King of Kings and Lord of Lords and He is Sovereign and He commands, and it happens.

What are you believing in God for? He shut the mouths of lions. He cursed a fig tree and it withered. He turned water into wine. He fed 5000 with just a few fish and loaves. He cast out demons. He created the universe. He knit you together in your mother's womb, and He loves you. I'll ask again, what are you believing God for? Because my God is able.

Memorize

"For I know that my redeemer liveth, and that He shall stand at the latter day upon the earth."

Job 19:25 KJV

Prayer

Lord, I love you and I love your word. Help me to fall more deeply in love with you and help me as I read today, to retain and understand what I am reading. I pray that you would speak to me through your word today and in this time of devotions.

Day 56

Spend today catching up on any days that you didn't get finished. It's important to enjoy God's word, and not to get overwhelmed if you fall behind, so today is a catch-up day, OR, if you are caught up, it's a good day to spend looking back at what the Lord has spoken to you about, or even spend this hour in prayer. Today is the last day of your memory verse, so you can spend some time with your memory verse.

"For I know that my redeemer liveth, and that He shall stand at the latter day upon the earth."

Job 19:25 KJV

Day 57

Read

Job 41 to Psalm 10

After Job had prayed for his friends, the LORD restored his fortunes and gave him twice as much as he had before. The LORD blessed the latter part of Job's life more than the former part. He had fourteen thousand sheep, six thousand camels, a thousand yoke of oxen, and a thousand donkeys. He also had seven sons and three daughters. The first daughter he named Jemimah, the second Keziah, and the third Keren-Happuch. Nowhere in all the land were there found women as beautiful as Job's daughters, and their father granted them an inheritance along with their brothers. After this, Job lived a hundred and forty years, he saw his children and their children to the fourth generation. And so, Job died, an old man and full of years. *Job 42:10 and 12-17 NIV*

We don't know how long Job suffered, but I have a feeling that Job remembered the goodness of God during his long lifetime, more than the suffering he went through. Scripture tells us that Job lived one hundred and forty years after all this. It also tells us that he had a full life. The Bible reminds us that although weeping remains for the night, joy does come in the morning. *Psalm 30:5.*

I have been through a few tough trials in my life, if you have ever heard my testimony, you kind of get the gest of some of it, but when I think of my life, I don't focus on what I lost, I focus on what I have. God will always give you more than you have ever lost or given us. That's His nature. God is good and loves us, and I trust Him with my life.

Can you think of a time when God came through in a big way after you endured trials? Thank Him for them now.

Memorize

"I know that thou canst do everything and that no thought can be withholden from thee"

Job 42:2 KJV

Prayer

Lord, I love you and I love your word. Help me to fall more deeply in love with you and help me as I read today, to retain and understand what I am reading. I pray that you would speak to me through your word today and in this time of devotions.

Day 58

Read

Psalm 11 to Psalm 27

Vindicate me, O LORD, for I have walked in my integrity, and I have trusted in the LORD without wavering. Prove me, O LORD and try me; test my heart and my mind. For your steadfast love is before my eyes, and I walk in your faithfulness. I do not sit with men of falsehood, nor do I consort with hypocrites. I hate the assembly of evildoers, and I will not sit with the wicked. I wash my hands in innocence and go around your altar, O LORD, proclaiming thanksgiving aloud and telling of your wondrous deeds. O LORD, I love the habitation of your house and the place where your glory dwells. Do not sweep my soul away with sinners, nor my life with bloodthirsty men, in whose hands are evil devices, and whose right hands are full of bribes. But as for me, I shall walk in my integrity; redeem me, and be gracious to me. My foot stands on level ground; in the great assembly, I will bless the LORD. – *Psalm 2*

David made it a choice to live a life of integrity. "Prove me, O LORD", he said. He gave God permission to speak into his life and test his heart and his mind. He made a choice to walk in God's faithfulness. He chose not to spend time with false people hypocrites or evildoers. This is a choice we need to make every day. We may have less friends when we let go of the ones who do not assist us in making the right choices, but we will have better friends. I heard a sermon years ago reminding us that who we are spending our time with, helps characterize who we are.

The sermon was about spending time with energy givers, (those who help you come closer to Christ), spending time with energy wasters, (they aren't necessarily bad, but they don't help you grow closer to Christ – they waste our time, you end up stagnant (fence sitters if you will) and spending time with energy suckers, (people who tear you away from Christ and help you make wrong choices). We only have so many years on this earth, but we get to spend eternity in the new heaven and new earth. Eternity with our Precious Heavenly Father, Eternity with King Jesus, who died, was buried and rose for us, Eternity with the Holy Spirit, who is our comforter, our teacher, our helper, who intercedes for us. I want the rest of my life to be the best of my life, like Paul, I want to finish well.

Are you spending your time with energy givers, energy wasters, or energy suckers? We become like those who we spend the most time with. Ask the Lord if you should be prioritizing your relationships. Don't waste your time on this earth, prepare now for eternity.

Memorize

"I know that thou canst do everything and that no thought can be withholden from thee"

Job 42:2 KJV

Prayer

Lord, I love you and I love your word. Help me to fall more deeply in love with you and help me as I read today, to retain and understand what I am reading. I pray that you would speak to me through your word today and in this time of devotions.

Day 59

Read

Psalm 28 to Psalm 44

As the deer pants for the flowing streams, so pants my soul for you O God. My soul thirsts for God for the living God. When shall I come and appear before God? My tears have been my food day and night, while they say to me all day long, "Where is your God?" These things I remember as I pour out my soul; how I would go with the throng and lead them in procession to the house of God with glad shouts and songs of praise, a multitude-keeping festival. Why are you cast down, O my soul, and who are you in turmoil with me? Hope in God for I shall again praise him, my salvation, and my God.

My soul is cast down within me; therefore, I remember you from the land of Jordan and of Hermon, from Mount Mizar. Deep calls to deep at the roar of your waterfalls; all your breakers and your waves have gone over me. By day the LORD commands his steadfast love, and at night his song is with me, a prayer to the God of my life. I say to God my rock; "Why have you forgotten me? Why do I go mourning because of the oppression of the enemy?"

As with a deadly wound in my bones, my adversaries taunt me, while they say to me all the day long, "Where is your God?" Why are you cast down O my soul, and why are you in turmoil with me?

Hope in God, for I shall again praise him, my salvation and my God.
– *Psalm 42*

This Psalm reminds us that God refreshes us and restores us when we spend time with him. David was thirsty for more of God. He knew his only hope was in God. He knew that in the midst of those who taunted him, only the LORD could satisfy his thirst, his need, his hope. This is going to happen if you serve the Lord and want more of Him in your life. People will taunt and tease. Especially when we are in our low times. Those who don't know the Lord, will say things like "Where is your God?"

"I thought you believed in God, where is He now?" But be like that deer that pants for the streams of water, seeking after the Lord. He is your salvation and the lifter of your soul. When you are cast down, Trust in the Lord.

God doesn't require us to understand what we are going through; he asks that we obey and glorify him. He wants us to see opportunities in our challenges. Sometimes in our challenges or trials, we get tired and discouraged. But like the deer, who knows to go to streams for its water, go to the Lord and allow Him to refresh you.

Memorize

"I know that thou canst do everything and that no thought can be withholden from thee"

Job 42:2 KJV

Prayer

Lord, I love you and I love your word. Help me to fall more deeply in love with you and help me as I read today, to retain and understand what I am reading. I pray that you would speak to me through your word today and in this time of devotions.

Day 60

Read

Psalm 45 to Psalm 69

Purge me with hyssop and I shall be clean; wash me, and I shall be whiter than snow. Let me hear joy and gladness; let the bones that you have broken rejoice. Hide your face from my sins and blot out all my iniquities. Create in me a clean heart, O God, and renew a right spirit within me. Cast me not away from your presence and take not your Holy Spirit from me; Restore to me the joy of your salvation and uphold me with a willing spirit. Then I will teach transgressors your ways, and sinners will return to you. *Psalm 51:7-13*

David knew that his sin separated him from God, but he acknowledged his sin by confessing and asking for forgiveness and asking God to restore to him the joy of His salvation. If you want to make a difference, then like David did, when he had sinned with Bathsheba and Uriah, repent, and be transparent.

No matter what we have done, we are never too far away from God. Jesus already died for that sin, we just have to confess our sins and repent. God is merciful and just to forgive us of our sins and then he cleanses us with His righteousness. While God is a just God, He does love us unconditionally.

If there is an unrepentant sin in your life or a sinful pattern that you are struggling with, God is Big enough. Take a moment to repent and allow God in all His mercy to cleanse you from all unrighteousness. Don't pretend. Let those in your realm of influence know you are not perfect. The Bible says to confess your sins to one another and pray for one another, that you may be healed. *James 5:16*

God assures us that while our relationship with him is personal, it's not private. Because we are a body, what we do in our private lives affects our brothers and sisters in Christ.

Memorize

"I know that thou canst do everything and that no thought can be withholden from thee."

Job 42:2 KJV

Prayer

Lord, I love you and I love your word. Help me to fall more deeply in love with you and help me as I read today, to retain and understand what I am reading. I pray that you would speak to me through your word today and in this time of devotions.

Day 61

Read

Psalm 70 to Psalm 80

We give thanks to you, O God; we give thanks, for your name is near. We recount your wondrous deeds. "At the set time that I appoint, I will judge with equity. When the earth totters and all its inhabitants, it is I who keep steady its pillars. I say to the boastful, 'Do not boast,' and to the wicked, 'Do not lift up your horn;'" *Psalm 75:1-4*

The Psalmist tells us to recount the Lord's wondrous deeds. Remember what the Lord has done. Moses told the Israelites to put things in the Ark of the Testimony to remind their descendants what the Lord had done for them. Jacob put a stone in the place where he wrestled with God. *Psalm 103:2* says Bless the Lord, O my soul, and forget not all his benefits.

Deuteronomy 5:15 says remember that you were a slave in the land of Egypt and Lord your God brought you out from there. *Psalm 77:11 says* I will remember the deeds of the Lord; yes, I will remember your wonders of old.

1 Chronicles 16:12 says Remember His marvelous works which He has done. God has done so much for us in our lives and He wants us to remember them, to remember His goodness.

What are some wonderful things He has done for you that you don't want to forget? Do you journal your thoughts? I love to write things down so that when I look back, I can recount all the wonderful things that God has done.

Memorize

"I know that thou canst do everything and that no thought can be withholden from thee."

Job 42:2 KJV

Prayer

Lord, I love you and I love your word. Help me to fall more deeply in love with you and help me as I read today, to retain and understand what I am reading. I pray that you would speak to me through your word today and in this time of devotions.

Day 62

Read

Psalm 81 to Psalm 96

He who dwells in the shelter of the Most High will abide in the shadow of the Almighty. I will say to the LORD, "My refuge and my fortress, my God, in whom I trust." For he will deliver you from the snare of the fowler and from the deadly pestilence. He will cover you with his pinions, and under his wings you will find refuge; his faithfulness is a shield and buckler. You will not fear the terror of the night, nor the arrow that flies by day, nor the pestilence that stalks in the darkness, nor the destruction that wastes at noonday. A thousand may fall at your side, ten thousand at your right hand, but it will not come near you. You will only look with your eyes and see the recompense of the wicked. *Psalm 91:1-8*

Moses wrote *Psalm 91* on the day, he completed the building of the Tabernacle in the desert. It was said to be written and recited reminding of God's protection over those who trust Him. Have you ever read a scripture that made you feel so safe and secure? I memorized this chapter when I was going through the worst trial of my life. It didn't change my situation, but it changed my heart throughout the situation. I recognized that nothing could come at me to do me harm without going through the Lord. That meant that I was in His will, no matter what the circumstances. During this very difficult, very trying time, I felt Him cover me with his pinion, and under His wings, I found refuge. God wants us to feel safe.

At a time when most people today live only for the moment, *Psalm 91* reminds us to put our trust in a God, who will never leave us.

Memorize

"I know that thou canst do everything and that no thought can be withholden from thee."

Job 42:2 KJV

Prayer

Lord, I love you and I love your word. Help me to fall more deeply in love with you and help me as I read today, to retain and understand what I am reading. I pray that you would speak to me through your word today and in this time of devotions.

Day 63

Spend today catching up on any days that you didn't get finished. It's important to enjoy God's word, and not to get overwhelmed if you fall behind, so today is a catch-up day, OR, if you are caught up, it's a good day to spend looking back at what the Lord has spoken to you about, or even spend this hour in prayer. Today is the last day of your memory verse, so you can spend some time with your memory verse.

Memorize

"I know that thou canst do everything and that no thought can be withholden from thee"

Job 42:2 KJV

Day 64

Read

Psalm 97 to Psalm 113

Give praise to the LORD, proclaim his name; make known among the nations what he has done. Sing to him, sing praises to him; tell of all his wondrous acts. Glory in his holy name; let the hearts of those who seek the LORD rejoice. Look to the LORD and his strength; seek his face always. Remember the wonders he has done, his miracles, and the judgments he pronounced. – *Psalm 105:1-5 NIV*

This Psalm is about the wonderful acts, wonders, and miracles of the Lord as he remembered his promises to his children. *Psalm 91* is full of worship and praise. The Psalmist is telling of all God's wonderful works. We discussed the importance of worship, we also discussed the importance of remembering God's goodness.

In this Psalm, the Psalmist reiterates the importance of both worshiping and remembering the good things God has done. "Remember the wondrous works that he has done, his miracles," the Psalmist said. We can never do this too often.

Psalm 91 was clearly written to call God's people to remember what He has done for them. Take some time to worship the Lord and remember His wondrous works in your life.

Memorize

"Thy word have I hid in mine heart, that I might not sin against thee."

Psalm 119: 11 KJV

Prayer

Lord, I love you and I love your word. Help me to fall more deeply in love with you and help me as I read today, to retain and understand what I am reading. I pray that you would speak to me through your word today and in this time of devotions.

Day 65

Read

Psalm 114 to Psalm 119

How can a young person stay on the path of purity? By living according to your word. I seek you with all my heart, do not let me stray from your commandments. I have hidden your word in my heart, that I might not sin against you. Praise be to you LORD; teach me your decrees. With my lips, I recount all the laws that come from your mouth. I rejoice in following your statues as one rejoices in great riches. I meditate on your precepts and consider your ways. I delight in your decrees; I will not neglect your word. – *Psalm 119: 9-16 NIV.*

A pure life is achieved by living in accordance with God's Word. Remember, if we want to love God's word, it is by spending more than a few minutes a day in His Word. We need to study His Word; we need to memorize God's Word. God's Word is powerful, God's word gives us direction. God's Word cleanses. We can delight in God's Word. I love the Psalms.

Psalm 119 is the longest chapter in the bible. It has 176 glorious verses. I love this portion of the Psalm. With my whole heart, I seek you... teach me your statutes... I declare all the rules of your mouth... I will meditate on your precepts... I WILL NOT FORGET YOUR WORD.

The way for us to stay pure is to be obedient to God's Word. We need to seek Him with all our hearts. We need to treasure His Word in our hearts. Let's take the time to declare the rules of the LORD, meditate on His precepts, and Not forget His word.

Memorize

"Thy word have I hid in mine heart, that I might not sin against thee."

Psalm 119: 11 KJV

Prayer

Lord, I love you and I love your word. Help me to fall more deeply in love with you and help me as I read today, to retain and understand what I am reading. I pray that you would speak to me through your word today and in this time of devotions.

Day 66

Read

Psalm 120 to Psalm 137

I lift up my eyes to the hills. From where does my help come? My help comes from the LORD who made heaven and earth. He will not let your foot be moved; he who keeps you will not slumber. Behold he who keeps Israel will neither slumber nor sleep. The LORD is your keeper; the LORD is your shade on your right hand. The sun shall not strike you by day, nor the moon by night. The LORD will keep you from all evil; he will keep your life. The LORD will keep you going out and your coming in from this forth and forever. – *Psalm 121*

Doesn't this chapter make you feel all warm and fuzzy? God never slumbers or sleeps, He is always available. The LORD will keep you forever. Talk about feeling safe in the LORD. I remember years ago, a friend of mine was due to have a baby and her husband traveled.

She asked if she could call me to take her to the hospital if she went into labor when her husband was away. I said yes. This was before cell phones. We had a land line and my land line rang and rang and rang and rang. I incorporated the ringing into a dream, then finally my husband said "Honey, the phone is ringing", I said okay and went back to sleep, then woke up with a start and realized that it was my friend. I called her back, and everything was fine. She told me that she was trying to call for 10 minutes. Aren't you glad that God isn't like that? He doesn't slumber or sleep. Psalm 46:1 says He is an ever-present help in trouble.

Psalm 121 reminds us God is our protector, that He is eternal, that He is in Control, and always present. When you are looking for help, lift up your eyes to the hills and see that your help comes from the Lord who made heaven and earth.

Memorize

"Thy word have I hid in mine heart, that I might not sin against thee."

Psalm 119: 11 KJV

Prayer

Lord, I love you and I love your word. Help me to fall more deeply in love with you and help me as I read today, to retain and understand what I am reading. I pray that you would speak to me through your word today and in this time of devotions.

Day 67

Read

Psalm 138 to Proverbs 5

My son, do not forget my teaching, but keep my commands in your heart, for they will prolong your life many years and bring you peace and prosperity. Let love and faithfulness never leave you; bind them around your neck, and write them on the tablet of your heart.

Then, you will wind favor and a good name in the sight of God and man. Trust in the LORD with all your heart and lean not on your own understanding; in all your ways submit to him and he will make your paths straight. Do not be wise in your own eyes; fear the LORD and shun evil. *Proverbs 3:1-7 NIV*

I remember going through a particularly hard trial in my life, and I was reading through the Psalms and Proverbs, looking for comfort and wisdom. That's usually where I go when I'm going through hard times.

I read *Proverbs 3:5-6.* "Trust in the LORD with all your heart, and do not lean on your own understanding. In all your ways acknowledge him, and he will make straight your paths." I read it again and again. I was devouring it. I broke it apart. This is what I did with those verses…

1. Trust.

2. Trust in the LORD.

3. Trust in the LORD with all your heart.

4. Do not lean on your own understanding.

5. Hmmm, that means don't look at my circumstances.

6. In all your ways acknowledge him.

7. Hmmm, only look to Christ.

8. Don't look at my circumstances, look to Christ.

9. Hmmm, set my affections on things above.

10. And he will make straight your paths.

This was the first time I realized what meditation really meant.

If you are going through a particularly difficult time in your life, find a scripture that speaks to you, and meditate on it. Read it, read it again, write it down, read it again, read it slowly, chew it up. This is meditation.

Memorize

"Thy word have I hid in mine heart, that I might not sin against thee."

Psalm 119: 11 KJV

Prayer

Lord, I love you and I love your word. Help me to fall more deeply in love with you and help me as I read today, to retain and understand what I am reading. I pray that you would speak to me through your word today and in this time of devotions.

Day 68

Read

Proverbs 6 to 17

The plans of the heart belong to man, but the answer of the tongue is from Jehovah. All the ways of a man are clean in his own eyes, but Jehovah weigheth the spirits. Commit thy works unto Jehovah, and thy purposes shall be established. Jehovah hath made everything for its own end; Yea, even the wicked for the day of evil. Every one that is proud in heart is an abomination to Jehovah: Though hand joins in hand, he shall not be unpunished. By mercy and truth, iniquity is atoned for; And by the fear of Jehovah, men depart from evil. When a man's ways please Jehovah, He maketh even his enemies to be at peace with him. Better is a little, with righteousness, than great revenues with injustice. A man's heart deviseth his way; But Jehovah directeth his steps. *Proverbs 16:1-9 ASV*

We can choose to do things our own way, and maybe fall and maybe make bad choices and maybe do okay, or we can ask the LORD for direction, and our plans will be established. Why?

The next verse says that the LORD has made everything for its purpose. God has a plan, he has a purpose for everything He does. Verse 9 is one of my favorite in the bible, In his heart, a man plans his course, but it is the LORD that directs his steps. Before I make decisions, I always pray and ask the LORD to direct my steps, this doesn't mean that I always make the right choices, but it does mean that if I make wrong choices, God will direct my steps. He will intervene. I choose to allow the LORD to establish my steps.

Are you ready to give the LORD permission to direct your steps? Are you ready to say, "Your way O LORD, not mine anymore."

Memorize

"Thy word have I hid in mine heart, that I might not sin against thee."

Psalm 119: 11 KJV

Prayer

Lord, I love you and I love your word. Help me to fall more deeply in love with you and help me as I read today, to retain and understand what I am reading. I pray that you would speak to me through your word today and in this time of devotions.

Day 69

Read

Proverbs 18 to31

Do not boast about tomorrow, for you do not know what a day may bring. Let another praise you, and not your own mouth, a stranger, and not your own lips. A stone is heavy, and sand is weighty, but a fool's provocation is heavier than both. Wrath is cruel, and anger is overwhelming, but who can stand before jealousy? Better is open rebuke than hidden love. Faithful are the wounds of a friend; profuse are the kisses of an enemy. *Proverbs 27:6*

Lately, the LORD has been convicting me about my pride. In going through the "Seeking Him" study (Nancy DeMoss Wolgemuth of Revive our Hearts), I am realizing that pride is an area of weakness in me.

One thing that I have realized is how important it is to have people speak into my life. I have such wonderful women in my life who I trust. I have one particular friend who, whenever we get together, we talk about the LORD for hours. We discuss what He is doing in our lives, in the church, and in the world.

One thing I am very thankful for is whenever I am in error about something, she loves me enough to correct me. Faithful are the wounds of a friend; profuse are the kisses of an enemy. I've had a lifetime of people telling me what I want to hear, but growth comes when someone loves you enough to tell you what you need to hear. This didn't just happen. We built a relationship of trust and honesty and then gave each other permission to speak into each other's lives.

Do you have a friendship like that? If you don't, ask the LORD to bring someone into your life, if you do, give them permission to be real and speak into your life.

Memorize

"Thy word have I hid in mine heart, that I might not sin against thee."

Psalm 119: 11 KJV

Prayer

Lord, I love you and I love your word. Help me to fall more deeply in love with you and help me as I read today, to retain and understand what I am reading. I pray that you would speak to me through your word today and in this time of devotions.

Day 70

Spend today catching up on any days that you didn't get finished. It's important to enjoy God's word, and not to get overwhelmed if you fall behind, so today is a catch-up day, OR, if you are caught up, it's a good day to spend looking back at what the Lord has spoken to you about, or even spend this hour in prayer. Today is the last day of your memory verse, so you can spend some time with your memory verse.

Memorize

"Thy word have I hid in mine heart, that I might not sin against thee."

Psalm 119: 11 KJV

Day 71

Read

Ecclesiastes 1 to Ecclesiastes 12

Not only was the Teacher wise, but he also imparted knowledge to the people. He pondered and searched out and set in order many proverbs. The Teacher searched to find just the right words, and what he wrote was upright and true. The words of the wise are like goads, their collected sayings like firmly embedded nails – given by one shepherd. Be warned, my son, of anything in addition to them. Of making many books there is no end, and much study wearies the body. Now all has been heard; here is the conclusion of the matter: Fear God and keep his commandments, for this is the duty of all mankind. For God will bring every deed into judgment, including every hidden thing, whether it is good or evil. *Ecclesiastes 12:9-14 NIV*

The author of Ecclesiastes starts off by saying "Vanity of vanities, all is vanity". Solomon had everything he could ever ask for. He had riches and wealth. He was so wise that the Queen of Sheba came a long distance to hear his wisdom. He was popular. And yet, he says it is all vanity.

Then he goes on to say in chapter 12, Fear God and keep his commandments, for this is the whole duty of man. If we have riches, fame, and wisdom, but have not the LORD, it's worth nothing. God commended Solomon at the beginning of his reign. He asked Solomon what he wanted, and Solomon asked for Wisdom. God said because you asked for Wisdom and not riches, I am going to give you both.

And yet, at the end of Solomon's life, his heart was led away from the LORD by his wives because he chose to marry women who didn't serve the LORD. Badcompany really does corrupt good morals. Ecclesiastes conveys the idea that the purpose of life is to fear God and keep his commandments, everything else is vanity.

To fear God means to submit your heart to God. Every area of your heart. Solomon did not submit his whole heart to God, he kept much of it back and gave it to his wives. He chose to spend his time and energy on the wrong people. Who are you spending time with? Do your relationships bring glory to God?

Memorize

For unto us a child is born, unto us a son is given; and the government will be upon his shoulder. And his name will be called Wonderful, Counselor, Mighty God, Everlasting Father, Prince of Peace.

Isaiah 9:6 KJV

Prayer

Lord, I love you and I love your word. Help me to fall more deeply in love with you and help me as I read today, to retain and understand what I am reading. I pray that you would speak to me through your word today and in this time of devotions.

Day 72

Read

Song of Solomon 1 to Isaiah 6

In the year that King Uzziah died, I saw the Lord sitting upon a throne, high and lifted up; and the train of his robe filled the temple. Above him stood the seraphim. Each had six wings: with two he covered his face, and with two he covered his feet, and with two he flew. And one called to another and said: "Holy, holy, holy is the LORD of hosts; the whole earth is full of his glory!" And the foundations of the thresholds shook at the voice of him who called, and the house was filled with smoke.

And I said: "Woe is me! For I am lost; for I am a man of unclean lips, and I dwell in the midst of a people of unclean lips; for my eyes have seen the King, the LORD of hosts!" Then, one of the seraphim flew to me, having in his hand a burning coal that he had taken with tongs from the altar. And he touched my mouth and said: "Behold, this has touched your lips; your guilt is taken away, and your sin atoned for." And I heard the voice of the Lord saying, "Whom shall I send, and who will go for us?" Then I said, "Here am I! Send me." And he said, "Go and say to this people…" *Isaiah 6:1-9*

It was a sad time for Isaiah. King Uzziah was a good King, but at the end of his life, he died of leprosy because he was vain. He couldn't handle his success and power. But then Isaiah had a vision, he had hope. God wanted to use Isaiah. After his lips are cleansed, Isaiah volunteers to take the Lord's message to his people Judah. The Lord shows Isaiah that the message will not be received but Isaiah says, "Here am I Lord, send me". It's hard sharing God's word with people who don't want to receive it, yet Isaiah was willing to go. Imagine how hard it would be if God said, "I want you to go and tell my people something, they won't listen, but I want you to go anyways.

This chapter describes Isaiah's call into ministry. God called Isaiah to give a message of warning but also of hope. It was a time of cleansing for Isaiah. God was prepping Isaiah for what he was asking of Isaiah. And Isaiah was willing. Are you willing to go where God has called you to go, to do what God has called you to do, to be who God has called you to be and to say what God has called you to say?

Memorize

For unto us a child is born, unto us a son is given; and the government will be upon his shoulder. And his name will be called Wonderful, Counselor, Mighty God, Everlasting Father, Prince of Peace.

Isaiah 9:6 KJV

Prayer

Lord, I love you and I love your word. Help me to fall more deeply in love with you and help me as I read today, to retain and understand what I am reading. I pray that you would speak to me through your word today and in this time of devotions.

Day 73

Read

Isaiah 7 to Isaiah 20

For unto us a child is born, unto us a son is given; and the government will be upon his shoulder. And his name will be called Wonderful, Counselor, Mighty God, Everlasting Father, Prince of Peace. – *Isaiah 9:6 KJV*

A scripture most of us have memorized, and we hear it often during the Christmas Advent services. But isn't it incredible? Approximately 740 years before the birth of Christ, Isaiah wrote about it. In an extremely dark period of punishment in Israel's history, Isaiah sees into the future and gives hope about deliverance. Isaiah is one of the most well-known prophets in the Bible. He predicted that the Lord would send the promised Messiah who would redeem his people from their sins. Isaiah revealed that this Messiah will be a child upon whose shoulders the government (dominion, sovereignty) will rest. Isaiah is a book filled with terrifying warnings of judgment and destruction while also giving hope with uplifting promises and prosperity.

This chapter reminds us that God had a perfect plan of redemption all along. He is Wonderful, He is our Counselor, He is our Mighty God, our Everlasting Father, and our Prince of Peace. He is also our Savior.

Memorize

For unto us a child is born, unto us a son is given; and the government will be upon his shoulder. And his name will be called Wonderful, Counselor, Mighty God, Everlasting Father, Prince of Peace.

Isaiah 9:6 KJV

Prayer

Lord, I love you and I love your word. Help me to fall more deeply in love with you and help me as I read today, to retain and understand what I am reading. I pray that you would speak to me through your word today and in this time of devotions.

Day 74

Read

Isaiah 21 to Isaiah 32

Behold, a king will reign in righteousness, and princes will rule in justice. Each will be like a hiding place from the wind, a shelter from the storm, like streams of water in a dry place, like the shade of a great rock in a weary land. Then the eyes of those who see will not be closed, and the ears of those who hear will give attention. The heart of the hasty will understand and know, and the tongue of the stammerers will hasten to speak distinctly.

The fool will no more be called noble, nor the scoundrel said to be honorable. For the fool speaks folly, and his heart is busy with iniquity, to practice ungodliness, to utter error concerning the LORD, to leave the craving of the hungry unsatisfied, and to deprive the thirsty of drink… But he who is noble plans noble things, and on noble things he stands. *Isaiah 32:1-6 and 8.*

In the aftermath of Jerusalem's deliverance, it was promised that a King would come, not just any king, but a king reigning in righteousness. God was letting them know that the Assyrians would be judged and that Judah would be delivered. God wanted to bless Judah with a righteous king, so he made the promise not only to remove the threat, but that deliverance was coming. Princes will rule with justice. In a time when God's people struggled with desolation and spiritual blindness, *Isaiah 32:1-2* promises that one day a king will rule over us who will be completely righteous, it is a reminder that Jesus will protect us.

While Isaiah 32 is a promise that referred specifically to the end time peace for the Jewish people, God's promise of peace applies to us today who choose to surrender their lives to the LORD.

Memorize

For unto us a child is born, unto us a son is given; and the government will be upon his shoulder. And his name will be called Wonderful, Counselor, Mighty God, Everlasting Father, Prince of Peace.

Isaiah 9:6 KJV

Prayer

Lord, I love you and I love your word. Help me to fall more deeply in love with you and help me as I read today, to retain and understand what I am reading. I pray that you would speak to me through your word today and in this time of devotions.

Day 75

Read

Isaiah 33 to Isaiah 44

In those days Hezekiah became ill and was at the point of death. The prophet Isaiah, son of Amoz went to him and said, "This is what the LORD says: Put your house in order, because you are going to die; you will not recover." Hezekiah turned his face to the wall and prayed to the LORD, "Remember, LORD, how I have walked before you faithfully and with wholehearted devotion and have done what is good in your eyes."

And Hezekiah wept bitterly. Then the word of the LORD came to Isaiah: "Go and tell Hezekiah, 'This is what the LORD, the God of your father David, says; I have heard your prayer and seen your tears; I will add fifteen years to your life. And I will deliver you and this city from the hand of the king of Assyria. I will defend this city. *Isaiah 38:1-6 NIV*

God was very gracious to Hezekiah, he told him that his death was coming and gave him an opportunity to put his house in order. The God's grace was extended even further. When Hezekiah cried and prayed and asked God to spare his life, God answered Hezekiah's prayer and told him that he would give him 15 more years. If Hezekiah hadn't prayed earnestly and asked the Lord to spare his life, he most assuredly would have died. Prayer matters, prayer makes a difference.

Are there things that matter to you that you haven't asked the Lord for? Take the time to pray now.

Memorize

For unto us a child is born, unto us a son is given; and the government will be upon his shoulder. And his name will be called Wonderful, Counselor, Mighty God, Everlasting Father, Prince of Peace.

Isaiah 9:6 KJV

Prayer

Lord, I love you and I love your word. Help me to fall more deeply in love with you and help me as I read today, to retain and understand what I am reading. I pray that you would speak to me through your word today and in this time of devotions.

Day 76

Read

Isaiah 45 to Isaiah 54

Thus says the LORD to his anointed, to Cyrus, whose right hand I have grasped, to subdue nations before him and to lose the belts of kings, to open doors before him that gates may not be closed; I will go before you and level the exalted places, I will break in pieces the doors of bronze and cut through the bars of iron, I will give you the treasures of darkness and the hoards in secret places, that you may know that it is I the LORD, the God of Israel, who call you by your name. For the sake of my servant Jacob, and Israel my chosen, I call you by your name, I name you, though you do not know me. I am the LORD, and there is no other, besides me, there is no God; I equip you, though you do not know me, that people may know, from the rising of the sun and from the west, that there is none besides me; I am the LORD, and there is no other. *Isaiah 45: 1-6*

When reading Isaiah 45, we see that the Jews will be free to return to Jerusalem. Isaiah declares that Cyrus (although a pagan) is being used by God; even so much as being called 'God's Anointed', that is 'Messiah'. Cyrus was a sympathetic leader and led his people with kindness and God used Cyrus to subdue nations before him and to strip kings of their armor, he chose him to open doors and gates. God was saying very clearly that there is no other God. The whole earth and everything in it is in the hands of the LORD. He can use anything or anyone He chooses to answer prayer and make a difference in our lives.

You are exactly where you are supposed to be. You were put in the family God chose for you, you are in the job, God called you to and you have all the gifts God gave to you. Everything in your life is in the hands of the LORD. He can use you to make a difference in someone else's life and He can use someone else to make a difference in your life.

Memorize

For unto us a child is born, unto us a son is given; and the government will be upon his shoulder. And his name will be called Wonderful, Counselor, Mighty God, Everlasting Father, Prince of Peace.

Isaiah 9:6 KJV

Prayer

Lord, I love you and I love your word. Help me to fall more deeply in love with you and help me as I read today, to retain and understand what I am reading. I pray that you would speak to me through your word today and in this time of devotions.

Day 77

Spend today catching up on any days that you didn't get finished. It's important to enjoy God's word, and not to get overwhelmed if you fall behind, so today is a catch-up day, OR, if you are caught up, it's a good day to spend looking back at what the Lord has spoken to you about, or even spend this hour in prayer. Today is the last day of your memory verse, so you can spend some time with your memory verse.

Memorize

For unto us a child is born, unto us a son is given; and the government will be upon his shoulder. And his name will be called Wonderful, Counselor, Mighty God, Everlasting Father, Prince of Peace.

Isaiah 9:6 KJV

Day 78

Read

Isaiah 56 to Isaiah 65

Arise, shine, for your light has come, and the glory of the LORD rises upon you. See, darkness covers the earth, and thick darkness is over the peoples, but the LORD rises upon you and his glory appears over you. Nations will come to your light, and kings to the brightness of your dawn. Lift up your eyes all about you; All assemble and come to you; your sons come from afar, and your daughters are carried on the hip. Then you will look and be radiant, your heart will throb and swell with joy; the wealth on the seas will be brought to you, to you the riches of the nations will come. – *Isaiah 60:1-5 NIV*

After darkness, God tells His people to arise and shine, because the light has finally come. This isn't a physical light, but the light that comes from the glory of the LORD. I think that is what God is calling us to do today. This is a dark time. God's people have oppression on all sides, but there has to be darkness before there can be light. God loves to shine His glory in the midst of the darkest times, so His people can see the contrast of darkness and light. God is saying in the midst of these dark times, arise and shine for the glory of the LORD has come.

Shine your light among your realm of influence so that people can see during these dark times, the glory of the LORD that has risen upon you.

Memorize

Before I formed thee in the belly I knew thee, and before thou camest forth out of the womb I sanctified thee, and I ordained thee a prophet unto the nations.

Jeremiah 1:5 KJV

Prayer

Lord, I love you and I love your word. Help me to fall more deeply in love with you and help me as I read today, to retain and understand what I am reading. I pray that you would speak to me through your word today and in this time of devotions.

Day 79

Read

Isaiah 66 to Jeremiah 8

Now the word of the LORD came to me, saying, "Before I formed you in the womb I knew you, and before you were born, I consecrated you; I appointed you a prophet to the nations." Then I said, "Ah, Lord GOD! Behold, I do not know how to speak, for I am only a youth." But the LORD said to me, "Do not say, 'I am only a youth'; for to all to whom I send you, you shall go, and whatever I command you, you shall speak. Do not be afraid of them, for I am with you to deliver you, declares the LORD." – *Jeremiah 1: 4-8*

I absolutely love this scripture. Before I formed you in the womb, I knew you. He appointed Jeremiah to be a prophet while he was in his mother's womb. God called you, He knows you, He formed you, and you are exactly where God appointed you to be. You are not a mistake. Everything you have gone through, are going through, and will ever go through, is for God's glory and for your good.

I spent years thinking that God made a mistake with me. I always thought that I wasn't enough. I needed to do more, to be more, but when I realized that God is a master creator that He doesn't make mistakes, and that He planned everything about me, (the family He put me in, the characteristics He gave me, the vessel He created for me, my gifts, my talents and even my lack thereof), I was able to be thankful.

Reflect on the truth that God is a good God, and He loves you. He not only formed you, He appointed you to be who you are today. As I said, He doesn't make mistakes, so as you reflect, remember His goodness, and be thankful.

Memorize

Before I formed thee in the belly I knew thee, and before thou camest forth out of the womb I sanctified thee, and I ordained thee a prophet unto the nations.

Jeremiah 1:5 KJV

Prayer

Lord, I love you and I love your word. Help me to fall more deeply in love with you and help me as I read today, to retain and understand what I am reading. I pray that you would speak to me through your word today and in this time of devotions.

Day 80

Read

Jeremiah 9 to Jeremiah 17

You are always righteous, LORD, when I bring a case before you. Yet I would speak with you about your justice: Why does the way of the wicked prosper? Why do all the faithless live at ease? You have planted them, and they have taken root; they grow and bear fruit. You are always on their lips but far from their hearts. Yet you know me, LORD; you see me and test my thoughts about you. Drag them off like sheep to be butchered! Set them apart for the day of slaughter! If you have raced with men on foot and they have worn you out, how can you compete with horses? If you stumble in a safe country, how will you manage in the thickets by the Jordan? Your relatives, members of your own family – even they have betrayed you; they have raised a loud cry against you. Do not trust them, though they speak well of you. *Jeremiah 12:1-3 and 5-6 NIV*

Jeremiah is so frustrated, this passage is basically about Jeremiah asking the LORD why good things happen to bad people but also, why bad things happen to good people. Jeremiah complains to God about the justice of God; He can't seem to reconcile the goodness of God with the prosperity of the wicked because of their hypocrisy, and he cries out to the LORD for his own uprightness. Jeremiah prays for God to destroy the wicked, not bless them. But God reminds Jeremiah that it is God who will deliver His people. God always has a plan, it is not necessary for God to reveal His plan to us, it is only necessary that we trust God to work out things for His glory and for our good.

We need to keep our affection on things above and remember to keep believing that God is good and that he never did the least wrong to any of his creatures. You can count on God, always.

Memorize

Before I formed thee in the belly I knew thee, and before thou camest forth out of the womb I sanctified thee, and I ordained thee a prophet unto the nations.

Jeremiah 1:5 KJV

Prayer

Lord, I love you and I love your word. Help me to fall more deeply in love with you and help me as I read today, to retain and understand what I am reading. I pray that you would speak to me through your word today and in this time of devotions.

Day 81

Read

Jeremiah 18 to Jeremiah 28

The word that came to Jeremiah from the LORD: "Arise, and go down to the potter's house, and there I will let you hear my words." So, I went down to the potter's house, and there he was working at his wheel. The vessel he was making of clay was spoiled in the potter's hand, and he reworked it into another vessel, as it seemed good to the potter to do.

Then, the work of the LORD came to me: "O house of Israel, can I not do with you as this potter has done? Declares the LORD. Behold, like the clay in the potter's hand, so are you in my hand, O house of Israel. – *Jeremiah 18:1-6*

What a beautiful picture of God and His people. God is Sovereign, and in His Sovereignty, he has the authority to form and fashion His people (us) as He pleases, when He pleases. Why did the Potter rework the clay? It was marred. It wasn't perfect. God, like the Potter, may choose to rework the clay (His people) because it is marred, because God has a purpose for His people, and it is His right to do so.

The potter did not throw away the vessel that he was working on, instead, he made it over again. God can take any rebellious life and make it into something useful. He can do it for you today if you allow him to.

Memorize

Before I formed thee in the belly I knew thee, and before thou camest forth out of the womb I sanctified thee, and I ordained thee a prophet unto the nations.

Jeremiah 1:5 KJV

Prayer

Lord, I love you and I love your word. Help me to fall more deeply in love with you and help me as I read today, to retain and understand what I am reading. I pray that you would speak to me through your word today and in this time of devotions.

Day 82

Read

Jeremiah 29 to Jeremiah 40

"At that time," declares the LORD, "I will be the God of all the families of Israel, and they will be my people." This is what the LORD says: "The people who survive the sword will find favor in the wilderness; I will come to give rest to Israel." The LORD appeared to us in the past, saying: "I have loved you with an everlasting love; I have drawn you with unfailing kindness. I will build you up again, and you, Virgin Israel, will be rebuilt. Again, you will take up your timbrels and go out to dance with the joyful.

– Jeremiah 31:1-4 NIV

God is promising that He will establish a new covenant with Israel because they have broken the old covenant. Jerusalem was broken, her houses vacant and in ruins. But the LORD says, "Again, I will build you and you shall be rebuilt." When we give our brokenness to God, He will make all things new.

God's desire for us to guard our hearts by focusing every area of our lives, our minds, will, and emotions, through His word. This study is about getting to know the word more, falling in love with the word, and walking in the word.

Memorize

Before I formed thee in the belly I knew thee, and before thou camest forth out of the womb I sanctified thee, and I ordained thee a prophet unto the nations.

Jeremiah 1:5 KJV

Prayer

Lord, I love you and I love your word. Help me to fall more deeply in love with you and help me as I read today, to retain and understand what I am reading. I pray that you would speak to me through your word today and in this time of devotions.

Day 83

Read

Jeremiah 41 to Jeremiah 48

The word that Jeremiah the prophet spoke to Baruch the son of Neriah, when he wrote these words in a book at the dictation of Jeremiah, in the fourth year of Jehoiakim the son of Josiah, king of Judah. "Thus says the LORD, the God of Israel, to you, O Baruch: You said, 'Woe is me! For the LORD has added sorrow to my pain. I am weary with my groaning, and I find no rest.' Thus, shall you say to him, thus says the LORD: Behold, what I have built I am breaking down, and what I have planted I am plucking up – that is, the whole land. And do you seek great things for yourself? See them not, for behold, I am bringing disaster upon all flesh, declares the LORD. But I will give you your life as a prize of war in all places to which you may go." – *Jeremiah 45: 1-5*

Baruch was the scribe for Jeremiah and although he was a faithful servant of the Lord, he complained about the sorrow and suffering he had been forced to endure while copying the scrolls of Jeremiah's prophecies. God heard Baruch's complaints and urged Baruch not to seek great things in this world. He should seek to be faithful to the LORD. He also promised through Jeremiah that He was planning to send great trouble to all the people on the earth, however, He promised that he would keep Baruch's life safe wherever he went. This is God's challenge and promise to us as well. He challenges us to seek to be faithful to the LORD, and he promises to keep us in His will.

The big idea here is not to serve God to seek good things for yourself, to serve God for who God is, for what He has done, and for what He will continue to do in your life.

Memorize

Before I formed thee in the belly I knew thee, and before thou camest forth out of the womb I sanctified thee, and I ordained thee a prophet unto the nations.

Jeremiah 1:5 KJV

Prayer

Lord, I love you and I love your word. Help me to fall more deeply in love with you and help me as I read today, to retain and understand what I am reading. I pray that you would speak to me through your word today and in this time of devotions.

Day 84

Spend today catching up on any days that you didn't get finished. It's important to enjoy God's word, and not to get overwhelmed if you fall behind, so today is a catch-up day, OR, if you are caught up, it's a good day to spend looking back at what the Lord has spoken to you about, or even spend this hour in prayer. Today is the last day of your memory verse, so you can spend some time with your memory verse.

Before I formed thee in the belly I knew thee, and before thou camest forth out of the womb I sanctified thee, and I ordained thee a prophet unto the nations.

Jeremiah 1:5 KJV

Day 85

Read

Jeremiah 49 to Lamentations 5

And thou hast removed my soul far off from peace; I forgot prosperity. And I said, my strength and my hope perish from the LORD: Remembering mine affliction and my misery, what wormwood and the gall. My soul hath them still in remembrance and is humbled in me. This I recall to my mind, therefore have, I hope. It is of the LORD's mercies that we are not consumed because his compassions fail not. They are new every morning: great is thy faithfulness. The LORD is my portion, saith my soul; therefore, will I hope in him. The LORD is good unto them that wait for him, to the soul that seeketh him. It is good that a man should both hope and quietly wait for the salvation of the LORD. – *Lamentations 3:17-26 KJV*

Jeremiah describes the desolation of the once proud city of Jerusalem. He is heartbroken over the devastation of the holy city. Jeremiah wrote the Book of Lamentations to remind us of the importance of mourning over sin. He reminds us that we must ask the Lord for forgiveness when we break his heart. But he also reminds us that though there are consequences to sin, if we place our trust in the LORD, we have hope.

This passage reminds us that we need to trust in the LORD even when we face the consequences of sin. But when we do sin, we need to mourn over that sin. We need to count the cost because it was costly. It cost the life of Jesus, the Son of God. How often do we take our forgiveness of sin for granted and forget that our LORD and Savior King Jesus, paid a huge cost for our sins? If you are struggling with sin in any area of your life, remember that someone paid a huge price to forgive those sins, and not to take that lightly. Give over to the LORD the areas that you are struggling with.

Memorize

It is the LORD's mercies that we are not consumed because his compassions fail not. They are new every morning: great is thy faithfulness.

Lamentations 3:22 & 23 KJV

Prayer

Lord, I love you and I love your word. Help me to fall more deeply in love with you and help me as I read today, to retain and understand what I am reading. I pray that you would speak to me through your word today and in this time of devotions.

Day 86

Read

Ezekiel 1 to Ezekiel 12

And he said to me, "Son of man, stand on your feet, and I will speak with you." And as he spoke to me, the Spirit entered into me and set me on my feet, and I heard him speaking to me. And he said to me, "Son of man, I send you to the people of Israel, to nations of rebels, who have rebelled against me. They and their fathers have transgressed against me to this very day. The descendants also are impudent and stubborn; I send you to them, and you shall say to them, 'Thus says the Lord GOD.'

And whether they hear or refuse to hear (for they are a rebellious house) they will know that a prophet has been among them. And you, son of man, be not afraid of them, nor be afraid of their words, though briers and thorns are with you and you sit on scorpions. Be not afraid of their words, nor be dismayed at their looks, for they are a rebellious house. And you shall speak my words to them, whether they hear or refuse to hear, for they are a rebellious house. – *Ezekiel 2:1-7*

Can you imagine receiving that calling in your life? I cannot imagine God saying "I am calling you to do something, and you might be successful, or you might not be successful. You might look like a fool, or you might not look like a fool, but hey, I'm calling you anyway." Well, that's kind of like the calling that Ezekiel received. God said, I am sending you to them, and they may or may not listen to you, and don't be nervous about how they look at you. And yet, Ezekiel said yes.

God wants us to be willing, when he calls, no matter what the outcome. You have probably had people with whom you have shared your faith, who mock you and your relationship with the LORD. That is never fun, but the bible says that the harvest is plentiful and the workers are few, pray therefore that the LORD will send laborers into the harvest *(Matt 9:37)*. There is so much to do and so few people to do the work so if God asks you to share you faith, when you know someone won't listen, or, if he asks you to do something but you know that it won't work out, there is a reason. Do it!

What has God asked you to do recently that has been difficult to swallow, but you know He asked you anyway?

Memorize

It is the LORD's mercies that we are not consumed because his compassions fail not. They are new every morning: great is thy faithfulness.

Lamentations 3:22 & 23 KJV

Prayer

Lord, I love you and I love your word. Help me to fall more deeply in love with you and help me as I read today, to retain and understand what I am reading. I pray that you would speak to me through your word today and in this time of devotions.

Day 87

Read

Ezekiel 13 to Ezekiel 18

The word of the LORD came to me: what do you people mean by quoting this proverb about the land of Israel: "The parents eat sour grapes, and the children's teeth are set on edge"?

"As surely as I live, declares the Sovereign LORD, you will no longer quote this proverb in Israel. For everyone belongs to me, the parent as well as the child – both alike belong to me. The one who sins is the one who will die." – *Ezekiel 18:1-4 NIV*

God makes it clear in Ezekiel 18, that a person is not going to be held accountable for the sins of his father. The world looks at a child brought up in a home of ungodliness and sees that child as a product of their upbringing.

I remember when I was young and in school going into a class for the first time, and the nuns looking at me and expecting the worst assuming I was following in the footsteps of my siblings and my parents. I remember one year making the choice that I would not be a victim of my circumstances. I made a choice not to follow in their footsteps. Just as some children can be brought up in a loving Christian home and can turn away from following the Lord, others can be brought up in an ungodly home and choose to follow the LORD. The choice is individual. That is what is being said in Ezekiel 18. We don't have the right to "blame it on our parents." The choice is ours on how we want to live our lives.

You are not the victim of your circumstances, Ezekiel taught that each person should only pay for their own sins. Take responsibility for your own challenges, and your own choices.

Memorize

It is the LORD's mercies that we are not consumed because his compassions fail not. They are new every morning: great is thy faithfulness.

Lamentations 3:22 & 23 KJV

Prayer

Lord, I love you and I love your word. Help me to fall more deeply in love with you and help me as I read today, to retain and understand what I am reading. I pray that you would speak to me through your word today and in this time of devotions.

Day 88

Read

Ezekiel 19 to Ezekiel 26

The word of the LORD came to me: "Son of man, set your face toward Jerusalem and preach against the sanctuaries. Prophesy against the land of Israel and say to the land of Israel, thus says the LORD: Behold, I am against you and will draw my sword from its sheath and will cut off from you both righteous and wicked. Because I will cut off from you both righteous and wicked, therefore my sword shall be drawn from its sheath against all flesh from south to north. And all flesh shall know that I am the LORD. I have drawn my sword from its sheath; it shall not be sheathed again. As for you son of man, groan; with breaking heart and bitter grief, groan before their eyes. And when they say to you, 'Why do you groan?' you shall say, 'Because of the news that it is coming. Every heart will melt, and all hands will be feeble; every spirit will faint, and all knees will be weak as water. Behold, it is coming, and it will be fulfilled, declares the Lord GOD. – *Ezekiel 21:1-7*

The Lord was about to cut off Jerusalem and the whole land to show his wrath against wicked and rebellious people. God tells Ezekiel to groan with a breaking heart and with bitter grief, to groan because he knows what is coming. God not only wants Ezekiel to tell his people but to lament for his people. To feel the pain that God obviously feels over the wickedness of his people. When we anguish over seeing sin, it changes our prayer life.

There have been many different things that God has used to change my life. Spending time in his word, worship, and community, but mostly prayer. Prayer changes who we are. When we spend time with the LORD, He makes a difference in our lives. If you don't have a powerful prayer life, it's never too late to start. The best way to get close to someone is to spend time with them, the best way to get close to the LORD is to spend time with Him, in prayer, in worship, in meditation, in reading His word.

Memorize

It is the LORD's mercies that we are not consumed because his compassions fail not. They are new every morning: great is thy faithfulness.

Lamentations 3:22 & 23 KJV

Prayer

Lord, I love you and I love your word. Help me to fall more deeply in love with you and help me as I read today, to retain and understand what I am reading. I pray that you would speak to me through your word today and in this time of devotions.

Day 89

Read

Ezekiel 27 to Ezekiel 37

Then he said to me, "Prophesy to these bones and say to them, "Dry bones, hear the word of the LORD! This is what the Sovereign LORD says to these bones: I will make breath enter you, and you will come to life. I will attach tendons to you and make flesh come upon you and cover you with skin; I will put breath in you and you will come to life. Then you will know that I am the LORD." So, I prophesied as I was commanded. And as I was prophesying, there was a noise, a rattling sound, and the bones came together, bone to bone. I looked, and tendons and flesh appeared on them and skin covered them, but there was no breath in them.

Then he said to me, "Prophesy to the breath, prophesy, son of man, and say to it, "This is what the Sovereign LORD says: Come breath, from the four winds and breathe into these slain, that they may live." So, I prophesied as he commanded me, and breath entered them; they came to life and stood up on their feet – a vast army. – *Ezekiel 37: 4-10 NIV*

This is a prophecy of the Jews' return back to their own land from captivity. I see so much more in this chapter, for instance... we have gone through years of a pandemic, and we are in dark times today, and yet, we can have hope that God is in control and can raise up an army out of dry bones. No matter what we are going through, we have hope that God is on His throne, and He is in control, and His will is going to be done, on earth as it is in Heaven.

We go through seasons of prosperity and seasons of dry bones. Remember to seek out the Lord in those dark times when we feel lost, to examine our own lives, and to line ourselves up with the one true God.

Memorize

It is the LORD's mercies that we are not consumed because his compassions fail not. They are new every morning: great is thy faithfulness.

Lamentations 3:22 & 23 KJV

Prayer

Lord, I love you and I love your word. Help me to fall more deeply in love with you and help me as I read today, to retain and understand what I am reading. I pray that you would speak to me through your word today and in this time of devotions.

Day 90

Read

Ezekiel 38 to Ezekiel 46

Then he led me to the gate, the gate facing east. And behold, the glory of the God of Israel was coming from the east. And the sound of His coming was like the sound of many waters, and the earth shone with His glory. And the vision I saw was just like the vision that I had seen when He came to destroy the city, and just like the vision that I had seen by the Chebar canal. And I fell on my face. As the glory of the LORD entered the temple by the gate facing east, the Spirit lifted me up and brought me into the inner court; and behold, the glory of the LORD filled the temple. – *Ezekiel 43:1-5*

This chapter contains Ezekiel's vision of God's glory returning to the temple. The rest of the chapter mentions God's promise to dwell there if His people will put away their sins and repent. How exciting when God shows up. That is an analogy I like to use whenever God does something amazing. God shows up. I remember when I used to work for Starbucks and had to be at work at 5 a.m. I did not like getting up that early, but God always loved to "Show up" on my way to work with the beautiful sunrise and a family of deer grazing in the middle of the field that I would drive slowly by. God loves to show off when He "shows up". I can just imagine how Ezekiel felt when he announced to the people that the glory of God was returning to the temple. The joy in that fact would have been amazing, but imagine being the bearer of that news. Do you get excited when God "shows up" and "shows off"?

Look for God to show up in the beauty of nature, the next rainbow, the sunrise or the sunset, or when you are going through something and He works it out for your good and for His glory.

Memorize

It is the LORD's mercies that we are not consumed because his compassions fail not. They are new every morning: great is thy faithfulness.

Lamentations 3:22 & 23 KJV

Prayer

Lord, I love you and I love your word. Help me to fall more deeply in love with you and help me as I read today, to retain and understand what I am reading. I pray that you would speak to me through your word today and in this time of devotions.

Day 91

Spend today catching up on any days that you didn't get finished. It's important to enjoy God's word, and not to get overwhelmed if you fall behind, so today is a catch-up day, OR, if you are caught up, it's a good day to spend looking back at what the Lord has spoken to you about, or even spend this hour in prayer. Today is the last day of your memory verse, so you can spend some time with your memory verse.

Memorize

It is the LORD's mercies that we are not consumed because his compassions fail not. They are new every morning: great is thy faithfulness.

Lamentations 3:22 & 23 KJV

Day 92

Read
Ezekiel 47 to Daniel 5

But Daniel made up his mind that he would not defile himself with the king's choice of food or with the wine which he drank; so he sought permission from the commander of the officials that he might not defile himself. Now, God granted Daniel favor and compassion in the sight of the commander of the officials. The commander of the officials said to Daniel, "I am afraid of my lord the king, who has allotted your food and your drink; for why should he see your faces looking gaunt in comparison to the youths who are your own age? Then you would make me forfeit my head to the king." But Daniel said to the overseer whom the commander of the officials had appointed over Daniel, Hananiah, Mishael, and Azariah, "Please put your servants to the test for ten days, and let us be given some vegetables to eat and water to drink.

Then let our appearance be examined in your presence and the appearance of the youths who are eating the king's choice food, and deal with your servants according to what you see." So he listened to them in this matter and put them to the test for ten days. At the end of ten days, their appearance seemed better, and they were fatter than all the youths who had been eating the king's choice of food. – *Daniel 1:8-15 NASB*

It is important to stand up for the truth, especially when faced with extreme pressure to give in to the world's ways. Days are coming when you will have to make a choice whether at work or among friends, but your choices will be challenged and you will have to decide whether you are going to stand up for what is right in God's eyes or give in to the pressure and choose to compromise.

We had those choices during Covid when we were told to close down our churches and worship in our own homes. This is totally contrary to God's law, and yet, most churches closed down. When we put our trust in the Lord, he will work all things out for His glory and for our good. He wants to. It didn't matter what the eunuchs said to Daniel, it says that Daniel had already resolved that he would not defile himself. It was a choice that he had made even before he was speaking with the eunuch. But because of his choice not to defile himself and to bring glory to the Lord, God blessed him. He and his friends were healthier than those eating and drinking the best from the king's table. When we make a choice to stand up with integrity and make the right choices, God will bless those choices.

Have you drawn your line in the sand? Have you made your choices ahead of time like Daniel did when he settled the matter in his own heart? The time to make those choices is not when the situation occurs, but beforehand, so that the matter is settled in your heart.

Memorize

I make a decree, that in every dominion of my kingdom, men tremble and fear before the God of Daniel: for he is the living God, and steadfast forever, and his kingdom that which shall not be destroyed, and his dominion shall be even unto the end.

Daniel 6:26 KJV

Prayer

Lord, I love you and I love your word. Help me to fall more deeply in love with you and help me as I read today, to retain and understand what I am reading. I pray that you would speak to me through your word today and in this time of devotions.

Day 93

Read

Daniel 6 to Hosea 6

Then the king commanded, and Daniel was brought and cast into the den of lions. The king declared to Daniel, "May your God, whom you serve continually, deliver you!" And a stone was brought and laid on the mouth of the den, and the king sealed it with his own signet and with the signet of his lords, that nothing might be changed concerning Daniel.

Then, the king went to his palace and spent the night fasting; no diversions were brought to him, and sleep fled from him. Then at the break of day, the king arose and went in haste to the den of lions. As he came near to the den where Daniel was, he cried out in a tone of anguish. The king declared to Daniel, "O Daniel, servant of the living God, has your God, whom you serve continually, been able to deliver you from the lions?" Then Daniel said to the king, "O king, live forever!" My God sent his angel and shut the lions' mouths, and they have not harmed me, because I was found blameless before him; and also before you, O king. I have done no harm."

Then the king was exceedingly glad and commanded that Daniel be taken up out of the den. So, Daniel was taken up out of the den, and no kind of harm was found on him because he had trusted in his God. And the king commanded, and those men who had maliciously accused Daniel were brought and cast into the den of lions – they, their children, and their wives... Then King Darius wrote to all the peoples, nations, and languages that dwell in all the earth; "Peace be multiplied to you. I make a decree that in all my royal dominion people are to tremble and fear before the God of Daniel, for He is the living God, enduring forever. *Daniel 6: 16-26 ESV*

Daniel had already made an impression on King Darius long before he was framed. In fact, this was why he was framed. Daniel had won the favor of the King. King Belshazzar was told, that there was a man in his kingdom whom is the spirit of the holy gods and then Darius had made Daniel one of three high officials with thoughts of promoting him above all the other officials. This ticked off the other high officials, after all, Daniel was a Hebrew, and not really part of them. But even though the officials framed Daniel, King Darius was upset and tried to think of a way to save him. When he couldn't come up with a plan, Daniel was thrown into the lion's den for worshipping and praying to the living God. But instead of anyone not serving King Darius being thrown into the lion's den, King Darius made a new ruling, that everyone MUST serve the God of Daniel, stating that He is the living God. Talk about reverse peer pressure. When we choose to stand up for righteousness, God can use us and make a difference in our realm of influence.

Are you known in your workplace, your neighbors, or among your friends as someone who stands up for truth? Are you succumbing to peer pressure in your realm of influence or do they know where you stand?

Memorize

I make a decree, that in every dominion of my kingdom, men tremble and fear before the God of Daniel: for he is the living God, and steadfast forever, and his kingdom that which shall not be destroyed, and his dominion shall be even unto the end.

Daniel 6:26 KJV

Prayer

Lord, I love you and I love your word. Help me to fall more deeply in love with you and help me as I read today, to retain and understand what I am reading. I pray that you would speak to me through your word today and in this time of devotions.

Day 94

Read

Hosea 6 to Amos 3

Hear this word that the LORD has spoken against you, sons of Israel, against the entire family which He brought up from the land of Egypt: "You only have I known among all the families of the earth; Therefore, I will punish you for all your wrongdoing." Do two people walk together unless they have agreed to meet? Does a lion roar in the forest when he has no prey? Does a young lion growl from his den unless he has captured something? Does a bird fall into a trap on the ground when there is no device in it? Does a trap spring up from the earth when it captures nothing at all? If a trumpet is blown in a city, will the people not tremble? If a disaster occurs in a city, has the LORD not brought it about?

Certainly, the Lord God does nothing unless He reveals His secret plan to His servants the prophets. A lion has roared! Who will not fear? The Lord God has spoken! Who can do anything but prophesy? Therefore, this is what the LORD God says: "An enemy, one surrounding the land, will take down your fortifications from you, and your citadels will be looted." - *Amos 3:1-8 and 11*

God's anger has been provoked due to his passion for justice and hatred for sin, and Amos was adamant that due to the oppression and injustice, God's judgment was going to come. Amos is underscoring God's Sovereignty and right to implement His will. The judgment that Amos announced was not a final judgment, but judgment from God is always about his relationship with his people. God is Just because he hates sin, and he desires a right relationship with his people, therefore, when he brings about judgment, it isn't for the sake of judgment alone as much as for the sake of repentance, bringing his people back to him.

In the same way, today, God's judgment still remains relevant for his people. Amos gives us a wonderful reminder about the God we serve, and how He still today reveals Himself to us.

Memorize

I make a decree, that in every dominion of my kingdom, men tremble and fear before the God of Daniel: for he is the living God, and steadfast forever, and his kingdom that which shall not be destroyed, and his dominion shall be even unto the end.

Daniel 6:26 KJV

Prayer

Lord, I love you and I love your word. Help me to fall more deeply in love with you and help me as I read today, to retain and understand what I am reading. I pray that you would speak to me through your word today and in this time of devotions.

Day 95

Read

Amos 4 to Jonah 4

Jonah had gone out and sat down at a place east of the city. There he made himself a shelter, sat in its shade, and waited to see what would happen to the city. Then the LORD God provided a leafy plant and made it grow up over Jonah to give shade for his head to ease his discomfort, and Jonah was very happy about the plant. But at dawn the next day God provided a worm, which chewed the plant so that it withered.

When the sun rose, God provided a scorching east wind, and the sun blazed on Jonah's head so that he grew faint. He wanted to die, and said "It would be better for me to die than to live." But God said to Jonah, "Is it right for you to be angry about the plant?" "It is," he said. "And I'm so angry I wish I were dead." But eh LORD said, "You have been concerned about this plant, though you did not tend it or make it grow. It sprang up overnight and died overnight. And should I not have concern for the great city of Nineveh, in which there are more than a hundred and twenty thousand people who cannot tell their right hand from their left – and also many animals?" – *Jonah 4:5-11 NIV*

Jonah had just seen a revival happen right before his eyes, 120,000 people repented and changed their ways, and Jonah was angry with God because they did not get their comeuppance. Have you ever had someone hurt you so much that you couldn't even pray for them, or when you did pray for them, you were hoping that God would give them what they deserved for hurting you?

After all, the bible says 'Beloved, never avenge yourselves, but leave it to the wrath of God, for it is written, "vengeance is mine, I will repay says the LORD" *(Romans 12:19).* And He does, but what if that person repents like Nineveh did, and all of heaven rejoices? I had someone in my life who hurt me deeply and betrayed my trust over and over again. The hardest thing was that this person never did ask for my forgiveness. It took a while to be able to start praying for them, but one day when I was reading the book of Jonah, it struck me that I was waiting for God to avenge me instead of praying that God would change this person and bring them back to Himself. This person isn't in my life anymore, but I will continue to pray for them because I know that God loves them. And if this person ever comes to the LORD, I will choose to rejoice with all of heaven when it happens. *(Luke 15:10)*

If there is someone in your life like that, are you able to pray for them, not that God repays them with vengeance for what they did to you, but that they turn from their wicked ways and repent and are able to ask forgiveness and are you able to rejoice with all of heaven when it happens? If so, then healing will begin in that area of hurt in your life.

Memorize

I make a decree, that in every dominion of my kingdom, men tremble and fear before the God of Daniel: for he is the living God, and steadfast forever, and his kingdom that which shall not be destroyed, and his dominion shall be even unto the end.

Daniel 6:26 KJV

Prayer

Lord, I love you and I love your word. Help me to fall more deeply in love with you and help me as I read today, to retain and understand what I am reading. I pray that you would speak to me through your word today and in this time of devotions.

Day 96

Read

Micah 1 to Habakkuk 3

Though the fig tree should not blossom, nor fruit be on the vines, the produce of the olive fail and the fields yield no food, the flock is cut off from the fold and there be no herd in the stalls, yet I will rejoice in the LORD; I will take joy in the God of my salvation. God, the Lord, is my strength; he makes my feet like the deer's; he makes me tread on my high places. – *Habakkuk 3:17-19*

I love the book of Habakkuk. He struggled with the same questions that people struggle with today.

1. God, where are you when I need you? *(Verses 1:1-1:11);*

2. Why do bad things happen to good people? *(Verses 1:12-2:4);*

3. Why do good things happen to bad people? *(Verses 2:4 -2:20)* and

4. Will I make it through this trial? *(Verses 3:1 to 3:19)* and then through it all, he ends the book by rejoicing in the LORD, knowing that no matter what happens, God is with him; that God is his strength; he is his salvation; and he WILL rejoice in the LORD. It's amazing how our attitude to our trials helps us through the trials. Will you make it through this trial?

Absolutely. How? By knowing that God is always with you, he is your strength and he is your salvation. And by considering it all joy when you encounter various trials, knowing that the testing of your faith produces endurance. And let endurance have its perfect result, so that you may be perfect and complete, lacking in nothing. (*James 1:2-4*)

Habakkuk made a choice to rejoice no matter what his circumstances were, are you able to do that? Are you able to rejoice in the LORD no matter what your circumstances are?

Memorize

I make a decree, that in every dominion of my kingdom, men tremble and fear before the God of Daniel: for he is the living God, and steadfast forever, and his kingdom that which shall not be destroyed, and his dominion shall be even unto the end.

Daniel 6:26 KJV

Prayer

Lord, I love you and I love your word. Help me to fall more deeply in love with you and help me as I read today, to retain and understand what I am reading. I pray that you would speak to me through your word today and in this time of devotions.

Day 97

Read

Zephaniah 1 to Zechariah 9

"Sing aloud, O daughter of Zion, shout, O Israel! Rejoice and exult with all your heart, O daughter of Jerusalem! The LORD has taken away the judgments against you; he has cleared away your enemies. The King of Israel, the LORD, is in your midst; you shall never again fear evil. On that day it shall be said to Jerusalem; "Fear not, O Zion; let not your hands grow weak. The LORD you God is in your midst, a mighty one who will save; he will rejoice over you with gladness; he will quiet you by His love; he will exult over you with loud singing. – *Zephaniah 3: 14-17*

Zephaniah spoke about God's justice and love for His people. God's justice comes from His passion to protect His people. God says He will heal and transform His rebellious people. Zephaniah warned the nations that the day of the Lord is near. God will judge the nations with a burning fire as he purifies them from sin. God loves His people and cares more about our souls than our circumstances. So, he comes in Judgement, but He also comes in Mercy and in Love.

This passage defines how God makes his people feel safe and secure in His love. Judgment is certain unless there is repentance. Only our repentance brings hope and restoration. Is there anything in your own life, that God is asking you to repent of?

Memorize

I make a decree, that in every dominion of my kingdom, men tremble and fear before the God of Daniel: for he is the living God, and steadfast forever, and his kingdom that which shall not be destroyed, and his dominion shall be even unto the end.

Daniel 6:26 KJV

Prayer

Lord, I love you and I love your word. Help me to fall more deeply in love with you and help me as I read today, to retain and understand what I am reading. I pray that you would speak to me through your word today and in this time of devotions.

Day 98

Spend today catching up on any days that you didn't get finished. It's important to enjoy God's word, and not to get overwhelmed if you fall behind, so today is a catch-up day, OR, if you are caught up, it's a good day to spend looking back at what the Lord has spoken to you about, or even spend this hour in prayer. Today is the last day of your memory verse, so you can spend some time with your memory verse.

Memorize

I make a decree, that in every dominion of my kingdom, men tremble and fear before the God of Daniel: for he is the living God, and steadfast forever, and his kingdom that which shall not be destroyed, and his dominion shall be even unto the end.

Daniel 6:26 KJV

Day 99

Read

Zechariah 10 to Malachi 4

"For behold, the day is coming, burning like a furnace, and all the arrogant and every evildoer will be chaff; and the day that is coming will set them ablaze," says the LORD of armies, "so that it will leave them neither root nor branches. But for you who fear My name, the sun of righteousness will rise with healing in its wings; and you will go forth and frolic like calves from the stall. And you will crush the wicked under the soles of your feet of the day that I am preparing," says the LORD of armies.

Remember the Law of Moses My servant, the statutes and ordinances which I commanded him in Horeb for all Israel. "Behold, I am going to send you Elijah the prophet before the coming of the great and terrible day of the LORD. He will turn the hearts of the fathers back to their children and the hearts of the children to their fathers so that I will not come and strike the land with complete destruction." – *Malachi 4 KJV.*

The book of Malachi, aptly coming at the very end of the Old Testament, sums up what the whole Hebrew Bible has been pointing to – god's people cannot be faithful to the covenant. The entire Old Testament shows that they've failed again and again. And though

God deals with their sin, He will not abandon them. He promised to redeem a remnant and sent a Messiah to fulfill his covenant promises. The final message? Another appeal for god's chosen people to return. God would prefer to see His people redeemed than to be destroyed when the end final comes. This chapter includes the ever-awaiting promise to send a messenger heralding the Messiah.

Malachi shows us how much God hates it when His people break His covenant. God loves covenant faithfulness. Today, Malachi would tell us to accept Jesus, love Jesus, and give our whole hearts to Jesus.

Memorize

"Let your light so shine before men, that they may see your good works and glorify your Father which is in heaven."

Matthew 5:16 KJV

Prayer

Lord, I love you and I love your word. Help me to fall more deeply in love with you and help me as I read today, to retain and understand what I am reading. I pray that you would speak to me through your word today and in this time of devotions.

Day 100

Read

Matthew 1 to Matthew 10

And he opened his mouth and taught them saying: "Blessed are the poor in spirit, for theirs is the kingdom of heaven? "Blessed are those who mourn, for they shall be comforted." "Blessed are the meek, for they shall inherit the earth." "Blessed are those who hunger and thirst for righteousness, for they shall be satisfied. ´ "Blessed are the merciful, for they shall receive mercy." "Blessed are the pure in heart, for they shall see God." "Blessed are the peacemakers, for they shall be called sons of God."

"Blessed are those who are persecuted for righteousness' sake, for theirs is the kingdom of heaven." "Blessed are you when others revile you and persecute you and utter all kinds of evil against you falsely on my account. Rejoice and be glad for your reward is great in heaven, for so they persecuted the prophets who were before you." – *Matthew 5:2-12*

Jesus set his ministry with the Beatitudes right at the beginning of his ministry. He didn't pull any punches. The Beatitudes teach us that we are blessed, even during trials. Why? Because we have eternity in Heaven, so no matter what we are going through, we know where we are heading. Jesus said if you want to be first, be last, be humble, be merciful, be hungry for righteousness, be meek, be pure in heart. Sum it all up? Be like me, Jesus said, be humble, and put others first. I pray all the time for God to help me to live like this. I pray continually that God will change me so that when people meet me, they will see fruit and know that I belong to Jesus.

Is there an area in your life you are lacking? Ask God who gives generously. Don't waste your prayers on things, ask the Lord to change you, and make you more like his son Jesus.

Memorize

"Let your light so shine before men, that they may see your good works and glorify your Father which is in heaven."

Matthew 5:16 KJV

Prayer

Lord, I love you and I love your word. Help me to fall more deeply in love with you and help me as I read today, to retain and understand what I am reading. I pray that you would speak to me through your word today and in this time of devotions.

Day 101

Read

Matthew 11 to Matthew 20

The kingdom of Heaven is like a treasure hidden in a field, which a man found and covered up. Then in his joy he goes and sells all that he has and buys that field. Again, the kingdom of Heaven is like a merchant in search of fine pearls, who, on finding one pearl of great value, went and sold all that he had and bought it. – *Matthew 13:44-45*

Is your relationship with the Lord worth that much to you? Are you willing to give up everything in your life just to have that relationship and to nurture that relationship and grow that relationship? It took losing so much in my life to realize that what I was holding on to was actually keeping me from growing in my relationship with the Lord to where I am today. When God asks us to put Him first in our lives, He knows it's because our lives will be 1000% richer and better than we could have ever imagined.

What are you holding on to that God is asking you to let loose? Is there anyone or anything in your life that you hold more dear than your relationship with the Lord? Ask Him to help you to put Him first. He loves you too much to be second in your life.

Memorize

"Let your light so shine before men, that they may see your good works and glorify your Father which is in heaven."

Matthew 5:16 KJV

Prayer

Lord, I love you and I love your word. Help me to fall more deeply in love with you and help me as I read today, to retain and understand what I am reading. I pray that you would speak to me through your word today and in this time of devotions.

Day 102

Read

Matthew 21 to Matthew 28

"At that time the kingdom of heaven will be like ten virgins who took their lamps and went out to meet the bridegroom. Five of them were foolish and five were wise. The foolish ones took their lamps but did not take any oil with them. The wise ones, however, took oil in jars along with their lamps. The bridegroom was a long time in coming, and they all became drowsy and fell asleep. At midnight the cry rang out: 'Here's the bridegroom! Come out to meet him!'

Then all the virgins woke up and trimmed their lamps. The foolish ones said to the wise, 'Give us some of your oil; our lamps are going out.'

'No', they replied, 'there may not be enough for both us and you. Instead, go to those who sell oil and buy some for yourselves.'

But while they were on their way to buy the oil, the bridegroom arrived. The virgins who were ready went in with him to the wedding banquet. And the door was shut. "Later the others also came. 'Lord, Lord', they said, 'open the door for us!'" But he replied, 'Truly I tell you, I don't know you.' "Therefore, keep watch, because you do not know the day or the hour." – *Matthew 25:1-13* NIV

This is a scary parable. All ten were virgins, all ten were waiting, all ten had their lamps, but five were foolish enough to forget to bring oil with them. This speaks to the character of the five. They were waiting, but were they ready? Jesus talks about the consequences of the carelessness of the five foolish virgins. This parable stresses the difference between those who are outwardly professing faith in Jesus, but some of them are nominal Christians (in name only) and inwardly don't really know him. As Matthew 7 says, "Lord Lord, did we not prophecy in your name and cast out demons in your name and do many mighty works in your name? And then will I declare to them, "Depart from me you workers of lawlessness. I never knew you". Oh to be ready when the Lord returns, to know Him, really know Him, and make Him the King on the throne of your heart.

This message urges us to always seek divine wisdom and keep our inner flame alive. Always be ready for Christ's return. The bible says to work out our salvation with fear and trembling. Our faith is not transferable; it cannot be shared with others. It must be our personal choice for our own personal faith.

Memorize

"Let your light so shine before men, that they may see your good works and glorify your Father which is in heaven."

Matthew 5:16 KJV

Prayer

Lord, I love you and I love your word. Help me to fall more deeply in love with you and help me as I read today, to retain and understand what I am reading. I pray that you would speak to me through your word today and in this time of devotions.

Day 103

Read

Mark 1 to Mark 8

And he said to them, "Is a lamp brought in to be put under a basket or under a bed, and not on a stand? For nothing is hidden except to be made manifest; nor is anything secret except to come to light. If anyone has ears to hear, let him hear." And he said to them, "Pay attention to what you hear; with the measure you use, it will be measured to you, and still more will be added to you. For to the one who has, more will be given, and from the one who has not, even what he has will be taken away." – *Mark 4: 21-25*

Again, we find Jesus talking about not hiding our light. The purpose of a lamp is to shine outward, not inward. If a lamp is put under a bed, it still illuminates but no one benefits from the light, at least not as many benefits from it. Jesus is saying, put your light on a lampstand so more people can see it. The lamp is your faith and the lampstand is Jesus. Jesus is encouraging his followers to stand out and to be an example, in other words, make a difference.

Jesus' last words before ascending to Heaven were to go and make disciples of all the nations, that can't be done by hiding our light. The bible also says that the harvest is plentiful but the workers are few. It doesn't sound to me, when I read God's word that shining our light is optional. It's a command from the LORD. Are you sharing what you have been given or are you keeping your light to yourself?

Memorize

"Let your light so shine before men, that they may see your good works and glorify your Father which is in heaven."

Matthew 5:16 KJV

Prayer

Lord, I love you and I love your word. Help me to fall more deeply in love with you and help me as I read today, to retain and understand what I am reading. I pray that you would speak to me through your word today and in this time of devotions.

Day 104

Read
Mark 9 to Luke 6

But I say to you who hear, love your enemies, do good to those who hate you, bless those who curse you, pray for those who abuse you. To one who strikes you on the cheek, offer the other also, and from one who takes away your cloak do not withhold your tunic either. Give to everyone who begs from you, and from one who takes away your goods do not demand them back. And as you wish that others would do to you, do so to them.

If you love those who love you, what benefit is that to you? For even sinners love those who love them. And if you do good to those who do good to you, what benefit is that to you? For even sinners do the same. And if you lend to those from whom you expect to receive, what credit is that to you? Even sinners lend to sinners, to get back the same amount. But love your enemies, and do good and lend expecting nothing in return, and your reward will be great, and you will be sons of the Most High, for he is kind to the ungrateful and the evil. Be merciful, even as your father is merciful. *–Luke 6:27-36*

Jesus didn't say that following Him was going to be easy. But this wasn't just a hard ask, it was impossible. But Jesus knew

221

that, He knew that on our own we couldn't do any of these things. He knew we would need Him, He also knew that He was going to have to leave us with the Holy Spirit because we were going to need help. But hey, Jesus did say that it was easier for a camel to go through the eye of a needle than for a rich man to enter the Kingdom of Heaven.

And when they asked how they could do it? He said, with man it is impossible, but with God all things are possible. This is why reading his word every day is so important, this is why praying every day is so important, this is why spending at least an hour a day with the LORD every day is so important. With man, it is impossible, but with God, all things are possible. We need God.

We are nearing the end of this 3-month challenge. Has it changed your love for the word? Has it changed your relationship with the LORD? Every day that we spend time with the LORD, it should be changing us. We need the LORD in every area of our lives, it isn't optional. He is the only one who can change you, He is the only one who can help you. He is your ever-present help in trouble.

Memorize

"Let your light so shine before men, that they may see your good works and glorify your Father which is in heaven."

Matthew 5:16 KJV

Prayer

Lord, I love you and I love your word. Help me to fall more deeply in love with you and help me as I read today, to retain and understand what I am reading. I pray that you would speak to me through your word today and in this time of devotions.

Day 105

Spend today catching up on any days that you didn't get finished. It's important to enjoy God's word, and not to get overwhelmed if you fall behind, so today is a catch-up day, OR, if you are caught up, it's a good day to spend looking back at what the Lord has spoken to you about, or even spend this hour in prayer. Today is the last day of your memory verse, so you can spend some time with your memory verse.

Memorize

"Let your light so shine before men, that they may see your good works and glorify your Father which is in heaven."

Matthew 5:16 KJV

Day 106

Read

Luke 7 to Luke 18

Now, it came to pass on a certain day, that he went into a ship with his disciples: and he said unto them, let us go over unto the other side of the lake. And they launched forth. But as they sailed, he fell asleep: and there came down a storm of wind on the lake; and they were filled with water, and were in jeopardy. And they came to him, and awoke him, saying, "Master, master, we perish."

Then he arose and rebuked the wind and the raging of the water: and they ceased, and there was a calm. And he said unto them, where is your faith? And they being afraid wondered, saying one to another, what manner of man is this! For he commandeth even the winds and water, and they obey him. – *Luke 8:22-25 KJV*

I have so many favorite books and passages in the bible, but one of my favorite is in Job, when God says to Job and his friends, "Who is this that darkens counsel by words without knowledge? Dress for action like a man; I will question you, where were you when I laid the foundation of the earth? Tell me, if you have understanding… Or who shut in the sea with doors when it burst out from the womb, when I made clouds its garment and thick darkness its swaddling band, and prescribed limits for it and set bars and doors, and said, 'Thus far shall you come and no farther. And here shall your proud waves be stayed. *(Job 38:1-4; 8-11).* Of course, Jesus can command the winds and the water, he created them. He gave them limits at the beginning of creation. He spoke and they were created, He spoke and they calmed. I love reading about God's Omnipotence.

Is it hard for you to believe that God can answer your prayers? He made the winds and the waves, he calmed the winds and the waves. He said Ask of me. God is all-powerful. What a mighty God we serve.

Memorize

"And David said concerning him, 'I foresaw the Lord before my face, for he is at my right hand, that I might not be shaken; therefore, my heart rejoiced, and my tongue was glad; Moreover my flesh also will rest in hope."

Acts 2:25,26 KJV

Prayer

Lord, I love you and I love your word. Help me to fall more deeply in love with you and help me as I read today, to retain and understand what I am reading. I pray that you would speak to me through your word today and in this time of devotions.

Day 107

Read

Luke 19 to John 2

He entered Jericho and was passing through. And there was a man named Zacchaeus. He was a chief tax collector and was rich. And he was seeking to see who Jesus was, but on account of the crowd he could not, because he was small of stature. So, he ran on ahead and climbed up into a sycamore tree to see him, for he was about to pass that way. And when Jesus came to the place, he looked up and said to him, "Zacchaeus, hurry and come down, for I must stay at your house today."

So, he hurried and came down and received him joyfully. And when they saw it, they all grumbled. "He has gone in to be the guest of a man who is a sinner." And Zacchaeus stood and said to the Lord, "Behold, Lord, the half of my goods I give to the poor. And if I have defrauded anyone of anything, I restore it fourfold." And Jesus said to him, "Today salvation has come to this house since he also is a son of Abraham. For the Son of Man came to seek and to save the lost." – *Luke 19:1-10*

I love it when God writes our stories, he gets it right up to the last detail. God knew that many years before Jesus was even sent to the earth, one day, he would be passing that way, and a sinner

227

named Zacchaeus, would need to be saved but would need help from the elements because he was a small man. Therefore, God made sure that seeds from a sycamore tree fell in just the perfect spot to grow so that Zacchaeus would have the best seat, so that at the perfect time, when Jesus looked up, he would see Zacchaeus sitting on the branch of that tree, and he would invite himself over for dinner and Zacchaeus' life would be changed forever. God loved Zacchaeus so much that he planted seeds, watered them, and nurtured them for that one day.

God loves you so much, and he has written your story. Nothing He has done or is doing is an accident. Everything God does has a purpose. You have no idea what he has planted to get you where you need to be.

Memorize

"And David said concerning him, 'I foresaw the Lord before my face, for he is at my right hand, that I might not be shaken; therefore, my heart rejoiced, and my tongue was glad; Moreover, my flesh also will rest in hope."

Acts 2:25,26 KJV

Prayer

Lord, I love you and I love your word. Help me to fall more deeply in love with you and help me as I read today, to retain and understand what I am reading. I pray that you would speak to me through your word today and in this time of devotions.

Day 108

Read

John 3 to John 11

For God so loved the world, that he gave his only Son, that whoever believes in him should not perish but have eternal life. For God did not send his Son into the world to condemn the world, but in order that the world might be saved through him. Whoever believes in him is not condemned, but whoever does not believe is condemned already because he has not believed in the name of the only Son of God. And this is the judgment: the light has come into the world and people loved the darkness rather than the light because their works were evil. *– John 3:16-19*

We only have 13 days left in order to get through the entire bible, and I am fairly certain that anyone taking this challenge has been called to eternal life with King Jesus, but let's ponder for a moment at this scripture. God love us (the world) so much (while we were yet sinners it says in *Romans 5:8)* that He gave his only Son. Jesus didn't come to condemn the world, but that through him, the world might be saved. Let's not take that life for granted. I hope that each one of us doing this challenge is drawing closer to the Lord through His word. That is my prayer for each one of you and is my prayer for myself. Lord, draw each of us closer to you.

Scripture tells us to work out our salvation with fear and trembling. It also says to make your election sure. We can know where we stand in our relationship with the LORD. Take this opportunity to ensure that you are right with God.

Memorize

"And David said concerning him, 'I foresaw the Lord before my face, for he is at my right hand, that I might not be shaken; therefore, my heart rejoiced, and my tongue was glad; Moreover, my flesh also will rest in hope."

Acts 2:25,26 KJV

Prayer

Lord, I love you and I love your word. Help me to fall more deeply in love with you and help me as I read today, to retain and understand what I am reading. I pray that you would speak to me through your word today and in this time of devotions.

Day 109

Read

John 12 to Acts 2

When they had finished breakfast, Jesus said to Simon Peter, "Simon, son of John, do you love me more than these?"

He said to him, "Yes Lord; you know that I love you." He said to him, "Fee my lambs." He said to him a second time, "Simon, son of John, do you love me?"

He said to him, "Yes, Lord; you know that I love you."

He said to him, "Tend my sheep." He said to him a third time, "Do you love me?" and he said to him, "Lord, you know everything; you now that I love you." Jesus said to him, "Feed my sheep. Truly, truly, I say to you, when you were young, you used to dress yourself and walk wherever you wanted, but when you are old, you will stretch out your hands, and another will dress you and carry you where you do not want to go." (This he said to show by what kind of death he was to glorify God). And after saying this he said to him, "Follow me." – *John 21:15-19*

Peter was putting his foot in his mouth more times than not. He must have felt like a screw-up. It's wonderful to see that no matter how many times Peter messed up, God still used him. Not only did God use him, but Peter ended up writing 2 books of the bible. It's possible that Jesus asked Peter if he loved him three times, reminding him that three times before this, Peter denied even knowing Jesus. Jesus knew the torment that Peter put himself through as soon as he heard the rooster crow the second time. It was all there when Jesus turned to look at him, which is why when he rose from the dead, the angel said "go and tell my disciples and Peter". Peter was his disciple, why name him? Because he knew how Peter was feeling, so he asked Peter three times, "Do you love me?" Why? Jesus is calling Peter to tenderly care for his people.

The thing that thrills me is that no matter how much you or I mess up, God can still use us. When we are sorry for our sins, God is faithful and just to forgive us our sins and to cleanse us from all unrighteousness. And then, he can use us mightily.

Memorize

"And David said concerning him, 'I foresaw the Lord before my face, for he is at my right hand, that I might not be shaken; therefore, my heart rejoiced, and my tongue was glad; Moreover, my flesh also will rest in hope."

Acts 2:25,26 KJV

Prayer

Lord, I love you and I love your word. Help me to fall more deeply

in love with you and help me as I read today, to retain and understand what I am reading. I pray that you would speak to me through your word today and in this time of devotions.

Day 110

Read

Acts 3 to Acts 15

Now when they heard these things they were enraged, and they ground their teeth at him. But he, full of the Holy Spirit, gazed into heaven and saw the glory of God, and Jesus standing at the right hand of God. And he said, "Behold I see the heavens opened and the Son of Man standing at the right hand of God." But they cried out with a loud voice and stopped their ears and rushed together at him.

Then, they cast him out of the city and stoned him. And the witnesses laid down their garments at the feet of a young man named Saul. And as they were stoning Stephen, he called out, "Lord Jesus, receive my spirit." And falling to his knees he cried out with a loud voice, "Lord, do not hold this sin against them." And when he had said this, he fell asleep. – *Acts 7: 54-60*

Stephen was the first Martyr in the New Testament. He didn't fight back, he didn't call them names, he knew that what was being done was going to be for glory of God. And how God was glorified through this man. How many of those men, throwing rocks at Stephen to kill him would have heard him say "Lord, do not hold this sin against them"? Someone obviously heard him because it ended up in the bible. To be able to say this is only possible if a person loves the Lord more than they love their family, their friends, yes, even their own life.

Knowing that God is Sovereign and therefore, nothing happens in our lives that God doesn't have a purpose for, gives us the courage to walk through anything we go through. It doesn't matter what we are going through, God is in control, God loves you and God has a purpose, therefore, it isn't trivial. Trust Him.

Memorize

"And David said concerning him, 'I foresaw the Lord before my face, for he is at my right hand, that I might not be shaken; therefore, my heart rejoiced, and my tongue was glad; Moreover, my flesh also will rest in hope."

Acts 2:25,26 KJV

Prayer

Lord, I love you and I love your word. Help me to fall more deeply in love with you and help me as I read today, to retain and understand what I am reading. I pray that you would speak to me through your word today and in this time of devotions.

Day 111

Read

Acts 16 to Acts 28

About midnight Paul and Silas were praying and singing hymns to God and the prisoners were listening to them, and suddenly there was a great earthquake, so the foundations of the prison were shaken. And immediately all the doors were opened, and everyone's bonds were unfastened.

When the jailer woke and saw that the prison doors were open, he drew his sword and was about to kill himself, supposing that the prisoners had escaped. But Paul cried with a loud voice, "Do not harm yourself, for we are all here." And the jailer called for lights and rushed in and trembling with fear he fell down before Paul and Silas. Then he brought them out and said, "Sirs, what must I do to be saved?" – *Acts 16: 25-30*

The Philippian Jailer didn't get saved because everyone was still there, (it being a close call) and he didn't get saved because of the miracle of everyone's chains coming off of them, no it goes further back than that. The Philippian Jailer received Jesus because, during their trials and tribulations, they continued to be an example of Christ.

It says about midnight, Paul and Silas were praying and

singing hymns to God and the prisoners were listening to them. They lived their faith in Christ whether in chains or free. It is when we are going through trials that people of looking at us, not when everything is going wonderful for us. We can all put a smile on our faces, and say "Praise you King Jesus" when the blessings are falling down on us. It's when the storms come and there is nothing left to hang on to but our hope in Jesus and we sing hymns and pray no matter what; that's when the people in our lives who are watching us, will start to believe. They will see that the Jesus you hang on to so tightly is actually worth hanging on to. "Consider it all joy," the Bible says when you face various trials.

I had someone in my realm of influence who would ask me how I was doing, and I would reply, God is Good, or something to that effect. One specific time, this person said to me, it's easy for you to be happy, everything in your life is going great. I just smiled at this individual and said, "Really? Do you mean like being in a car accident 7 years ago and living with chronic pain? Or like being married for 40 years to a man who cheated on me and told my children that he never loved me? You mean that kind of great?"

This individual had nothing else to say because they realized that my joy is not because of my circumstances, it's not because everything in my life is going great. It's because I made a choice to consider it all joy when I face various trials. It's because of Jesus. We can be a bigger witness through our trials than on our mountain tops. Draw your line in the sand now that no matter what you are going through, God is your joy and your witness. Decide now to consider it all joy when you face various trials.

Memorize

"And David said concerning him, 'I foresaw the Lord before my face, for he is at my right hand, that I might not be shaken; therefore, my heart rejoiced, and my tongue was glad; Moreover, my flesh also will rest in hope.'"

Acts 2:25,26 KJV

Prayer

Lord, I love you and I love your word. Help me to fall more deeply in love with you and help me as I read today, to retain and understand what I am reading. I pray that you would speak to me through your word today and in this time of devotions.

Day 112

Spend today catching up on any days that you didn't get finished. It's important to enjoy God's word, and not to get overwhelmed if you fall behind, so today is a catch-up day, OR, if you are caught up, it's a good day to spend looking back at what the Lord has spoken to you about, or even spend this hour in prayer. Today is the last day of your memory verse, so you can spend some time with your memory verse.

Memorize

"And David said concerning him, 'I foresaw the Lord before my face, for he is at my right hand, that I might not be shaken; therefore, my heart rejoiced, and my tongue was glad; Moreover, my flesh also will rest in hope."

Acts 2:25,26 KJV

Day 113

Read

Romans 1 to Romans 16

Therefore, I urge you, brothers and sisters, in view of God's mercy, to offer your bodies as a living sacrifice, holy and pleasing to God – this is your true and proper worship. Do not conform to the pattern of this world but be transformed by the renewing of your mind. Then you will be able to test and approve what God's will is – his good, pleasing, and perfect will. – *Romans 12:1-2 NIV*

What does it mean to present your body as a living sacrifice, holy and acceptable to God? It means that we shouldn't be the same as the world is and that we should allow God to change the way we think. It's about living a life of worship to God through personal sacrifice and holiness. God doesn't want us to think the way the world thinks, he wants us to think the way He thinks. Romans goes on to explain what these verses mean, "be transformed by renewing your mind".

In other words, be Heavenly minded. "Set your affections on things above, not on things on this earth" (*Colossians 3:2*). We must live our lives in a continual state of surrender and consecration.

Romans 12 encourages us to reflect and renew our minds. It is only through the commitment to live our lives in God's perfect will that we can have true joy.

Memorize

"But the fruit of the Spirit is love, joy, peace, patience, kindness, goodness, faithfulness, gentleness, and self-control; against such things there is no law."

Galatians 5:22-24 ESV

Prayer

Lord, I love you and I love your word. Help me to fall more deeply in love with you and help me as I read today, to retain and understand what I am reading. I pray that you would speak to me through your word today and in this time of devotions.

Day 114

Read

1 Corinthians 1 to 1 Corinthians 15

I give thanks to my God always for you because of the grace of God that was given you in Christ Jesus, that in every way you were enriched in him in all speech and all knowledge, even as the testimony about Christ was confirmed among you so that you are not lacking in any spiritual gift, as you wait for the revealing of our Lord Jesus Christ, who will sustain you to the end, guiltless in the day of our Lord Jesus Christ. God is faithful by whom you were called into the fellowship of his Son Jesus Christ our Lord. – *1 Corinthians 1:4-9*

Paul was so encouraged that God had used him to bring the gospel to so many. His relationship with the churches he helped form didn't stop at their receiving the Lord, but much of the New Testament is built on his continued relationship with the churches he started. His letters of admonishing, rebuking, loving, and caring are what we read daily, and which help us even today to walk according to the practices that he taught and which God called us to follow. When we lead others to the Lord, it is important that we continue to pray for them and connect with them to ensure that they are not struggling in their walk with the Lord.

God wants to use us to make a difference for His Kingdom. I always felt that God gave me two hands to be His hands extended here on earth. God commanded us to go to all the earth and preach the gospel. It wasn't a request; it was a command. So that doesn't necessarily mean that we are to travel to be God's hands extended, it could mean to share the gospel with co-workers, friends, neighbors, and family. Allow God to use you in your realm of influence. Ask Him what that looks like. And then like Paul, be encouraged that God used you to share the gospel with so many.

Memorize

"But the fruit of the Spirit is love, joy, peace, patience, kindness, goodness, faithfulness, gentleness, and self-control; against such things there is no law."

Galatians 5:22-24 ESV

Prayer

Lord, I love you and I love your word. Help me to fall more deeply in love with you and help me as I read today, to retain and understand what I am reading. I pray that you would speak to me through your word today and in this time of devotions.

Day 115

Read

1 Corinthians 16 to 2 Corinthians 13

If I speak in the tongues of men and of angels but have no love, I am a noisy gong or a clanging cymbal. And if I have prophetic powers, and understand all mysteries and all knowledge, and if I have all faith, so as to remove mountains, but have not love, I am nothing. "Love is patient and kind; love does not envy or boast, it is not arrogant or rude. It does not insist on its own way; it is not irritable or resentful; it does not rejoice at wrongdoing but rejoices with the truth. Love bears all things, believes all things, hopes all things, endures all things. Love never ends. – *1 Corinthians 13:1-8*

The NIV version reads like this in verse 5, "love keeps no record of wrongs." I love that. This chapter shows us how to love one another. The bible says the greatest commandment is to "love the Lord your God with all your heart and soul and mind and strength, and the second is this, to love your neighbor as yourself."

Mark 12:30 and 31 says there is no commandment greater than these. So, if that is true, we need to learn how to love. 1 Corinthians 13 is a map of how to do just that. Love is patient, kind, humble, forgiving, and keeps no record of wrongs. We not only forgive, but we wipe the slate clean. That doesn't mean you go back for more abuse, but you remove it from your ledger. I pray every day that the Lord will help me to love more. I'll end it here because tomorrow we will be reading about the fruit of the spirit. But let's learn how to love better.

Love is an action word. It involves putting the other person's best interests first. Biblical love is permanent. God's love never fails. Make a choice to love, love and when there is nothing else to give, love some more.

Memorize

"But the fruit of the Spirit is love, joy, peace, patience, kindness, goodness, faithfulness, gentleness, and self-control; against such things there is no law."

Galatians 5:22-24 ESV

Prayer

Lord, I love you and I love your word. Help me to fall more deeply in love with you and help me as I read today, to retain and understand what I am reading. I pray that you would speak to me through your word today and in this time of devotions.

Day 116

Read

Galatians 1 to Philippians 4

But I say, walk by the Spirit, and you will not gratify the desires of the flesh. For the desires of the flesh are against the Spirit, and the desires of the Spirit are against the flesh, for these are opposed to each other, to keep you from doing the things you want to do... But the fruit of the Spirit is love, joy, peace, patience, kindness, goodness, faithfulness, gentleness, self-control; against such things, there is no law. And those who belong to Christ Jesus have crucified the flesh with its passions and desires. – *Galatians 5:16-17, 22-24*

Yesterday we talked about 1 Corinthians 13 being the road map to teach us how to love, Galatians gives us test points. The bible says you will know them by their fruit. What fruit? The fruit of the spirit. Are you walking in love with others? Do people see you being full of the Joy of the Lord? Are you a peace maker or are you one to stir up strife and dissension? Are you patient or do you get angry easily? Are you kind to others (not just those you like)? Are you a good person? Are you faithful in your relationship with the Lord and with others? Are you gentle in your dealings with others? Do you exhibit self-control?

Again, I pray every day and ask the Lord to help me in every one of these areas. I want to be more loving. I want others to see the Joy of the Lord in my life. I want to be a peace maker. I want to be patient when someone wrongs me. I want to be kind to everyone. I want to be known as a good person. I want to be faithful in my relationship with God and others. I want to be gentle. I want to exhibit self-control. I can't do any of this on my own. But I pray every day and ask the Lord to help me in every area. I want others to see Jesus in me, and if I am walking in the fruit of the spirit, they will. Do I screw up? Absolutely. Every day. But every day, there is more fruit, because I have asked the Lord to change me.

Do they know you by your fruit? How is your fruit? Are you someone who gave to the hungry, invited in a stranger, clothed someone in need, helped the sick and those in prison? Jesus said whatever you do for the least of these, you do for me. I'll ask again, how is your fruit?

Memorize

"But the fruit of the Spirit is love, joy, peace, patience, kindness, goodness, faithfulness, gentleness, and self-control; against such things there is no law."

Galatians 5:22-24 ESV

Prayer

Lord, I love you and I love your word. Help me to fall more deeply in love with you and help me as I read today, to retain and understand what I am reading. I pray that you would speak to me through your word today and in this time of devotions.

Day 117

Read

Colossians 1 to 1 Timothy 2

If then you have been raised with Christ, seek the things that are above where Christ is, seated at the right hand of God. Set your mind on things that are above, not on things that are on earth. For you have died, and your life is hidden with Christ in God. When Christ who is your life appears, then you also will appear with him in glory. Put to death therefore what is earthly in you. – *Colossians 3:1-5*

Set your mind (affections) on things above, not on things that are on earth. There is only one way to do that. Let me give you an example. I have never had a desire to visit Alberta. It's cold and I'm not fond of flying and I'm a home body. But a couple of years ago, my daughter moved to Alberta, now I have been there multiple times and I love it. I am planning to go again in a couple of months, and I can't wait.

Why? Because I love and miss my daughter. I think about seeing her all the time. If Christ is our affection, then it makes it easier to think about the things above. Even more than my desire to go to Alberta and see my daughter, is my desire to go to Heaven and see my God. I think about Heaven all the time. I think about being with the Lord and being free from this painful body and sinful world and being with Him. However, I know that He has a plan and a purpose for me to remain on earth. So, for now, all I can do is set my mind on things above not on things on the earth, and spend as much time with Him in my devotional time and throughout the day and ask Him what He wants me to do here on earth. I pray they will be done on earth as it is in Heaven.

Are your affections set on the things above? Are you heavenly-minded? Or earthly-minded?

Memorize

"But the fruit of the Spirit is love, joy, peace, patience, kindness, goodness, faithfulness, gentleness, and self-control; against such things there is no law."

Galatians 5:22-24 ESV

Prayer

Lord, I love you and I love your word. Help me to fall more deeply in love with you and help me as I read today, to retain and understand what I am reading. I pray that you would speak to me through your word today and in this time of devotions.

Day 118

Read

1 Timothy 3 to Hebrews 4

So, do not be ashamed of the testimony about our Lord or of me his prisoner. Rather, join with me in suffering for the gospel, by the power of God. He has saved us and called us to a holy life – not because of anything we have done but because of his own purpose and grace. This grace was given to us in Christ Jesus before the beginning of time, but it has now been revealed through the appearing of our Savior, Christ Jesus, who has destroyed death and has brought life and immortality to light through the gospel.

And of this gospel, I was appointed a herald and an apostle and a teacher. That is why I am suffering as I am. Yet this is no cause for shame, because I know whom I have believed, and am convinced that he is able to guard what I have entrusted to him until that day. – *2 Timothy 1:8-12 NIV*

God has a plan and purpose for each of our lives. He wrote your story. And he wrote it for His glory and for your good. He called us to a holy calling because of His own purpose and grace. He called us before the ages began. When I am going through trials and hurts in my life, I think of this. God has written my story. God doesn't make mistakes. God loves me. God is a good God. Why fear? These are other ways to set our affections on things above. Think about these things. Think about His goodness. Think about His love for you. Think about how he doesn't make mistakes. When we think about these things, we can go through anything, knowing He is in control.

You can trust God in every area of your life. Trust him with your life, with your marriage, with your children, with your ministry, with your health, with your job. Trust him totally with every area of your life.

Memorize

"But the fruit of the Spirit is love, joy, peace, patience, kindness, goodness, faithfulness, gentleness, and self-control; against such things there is no law."

Galatians 5:22-24 ESV

Prayer

Lord, I love you and I love your word. Help me to fall more deeply in love with you and help me as I read today, to retain and understand what I am reading. I pray that you would speak to me through your word today and in this time of devotions.

Day 119

Read

Hebrews 5 to 1 Peter 1

Now faith is the assurance of things hoped for, the conviction of things not seen. For by it, the people of old received their commendation. By faith we understand that the universe was created by the word of God, so that what is seen was not made out of things are visible. By faith, Abel offered to God a more acceptable sacrifice than Cain... By faith, Enoch was taken up so that he should not see death... By faith Noah, being warned by God concerning events as yet unseen constructed an ark for the saving of his household... By faith, Abraham obeyed when he was called to go out to a place that he was to receive as an inheritance... By faith, Sarah herself received power to conceive... By faith Abraham, when he was tested, offered up Isaac... By faith Jacob, when dying blessed each of the sons of Joseph... By faith Joseph, at the end of his life, made mention of the exodus of the Israelites... By faith, Moses was hidden for three months by his parents... By faith Moses refused to be called the son of Pharaoh's daughter, choosing rather to be mistreated by the people of God... By faith, the people crossed the Red Sea... By faith, the walls of Jericho came down... - *Hebrews 11:1-30*

Wow, what a great chapter. I love Superhero movies. I love all the Marvel movies. My favorite Superhero is Captain America. But when I read this chapter, which is called the Bible Hall of fame, so full of the heroes of our faith, I recognize that Captain America has nothing on them. *Hebrews 12:1* then goes on to say "Therefore, since we are surrounded by so great a cloud of witnesses, (the heroes of our faith) let us also lay aside every weight and sin which clings so closely and let us run with endurance the race that is set before us, looking to Jesus, the founder and perfector of our faith.

The 11th chapter of Hebrews is the greatest Hall of Fame we could ever look at. I can't wait to meet all of these great men and women who by faith believed in greater things. Just as those who've gone before us, I pray that those who come behind us, find us faithful.

Who is your favorite Superhero? And when I ask that question, I don't mean the Hollywood ones, I mean from scripture. Is it Daniel who was in the Lion's Den? Is it Sarah or believed God for the great miracle of life in her old age? The bible says that God never changes, so He is the same God today as He was when Daniel was in the Lion's den, when Sarah conceived in her old age and when Noah and his family were saved from the flood. He is the same yesterday, today, and forever. Just like our heroes of old, God can do it again and wants to. Allow Him to work in your life.

Memorize

"But the fruit of the Spirit is love, joy, peace, patience, kindness, goodness, faithfulness, gentleness, and self-control; against such things there is no law."

Galatians 5:22-24 ESV

Prayer

Lord, I love you and I love your word. Help me to fall more deeply in love with you and help me as I read today, to retain and understand what I am reading. I pray that you would speak to me through your word today and in this time of devotions.

Day 120

Read

1 Peter 2 to Revelation 3

Dear friends, let us love one another, for love comes from God. Everyone who loves has been born of God and knows God. Whoever does not love does not know God, because God is love. This is how God showed his love among us: He sent his one and only son into the world that we might live through him.

This is love: not that we loved God, but that he loved us and sent his Son as an atoning sacrifice for our sins. Dear friends, since God so loved us, we also ought to love one another. No one has ever seen God; but if we love one another, God lives in us and his love is made complete in us. This is how we know that we live in him and he in us: He has given us his Spirit. *– 1 John 4: 7-13 NIV*

Here we go again, talking about love. If God loves us so much that He sent His Son, then yes, we ought to love one another. John knew Jesus' love for him. He called himself 'the disciple whom Jesus loved' (see *John 13:23*) throughout his gospel. We have talked about loving others, and yes, the bible commands that we love one another. This is the second last day of our challenge. I want to ensure that we all know how much God loves us. I want to know His love for me so much that I can say as John does, 'I am Suzanne, the one who Jesus loves'. We all need to know deep in our hearts that love. Let's focus on God's love for us. Let it penetrate our beings. Meditate on His love for you. We love him because He first loved us.

Take this time to solidify your love for the LORD, remembering that you love Him because He first loved us. In fact, it is when we were sinners, at our very worst, that Christ died for us.

Memorize

"But the fruit of the Spirit is love, joy, peace, patience, kindness, goodness, faithfulness, gentleness, and self-control; against such things there is no law."

Galatians 5:22-24 ESV

Prayer

Lord, I love you and I love your word. Help me to fall more deeply in love with you and help me as I read today, to retain and understand what I am reading. I pray that you would speak to me through your word today and in this time of devotions.

Day 121

Read

Revelation 4 to Revelation 22

Then, I saw a new heaven and a new earth, for the first heaven and the first earth had passed away, and the sea was no more. And I saw the holy city, new Jerusalem, coming down out of haven from God, prepared as a bride adorned for her husband.

And I heard a loud voice from the throne saying, "Behold, the dwelling place of God is with man. He will dwell with them, and they will be his people, and God himself will be with them as their god. He will wipe away every tear from their eyes, and death shall be no more, neither shall there be mourning, nor crying, nor pain anymore for the former things have passed away." – *Revelation 21:1-4*

Revelation 21 describes a time when God's domain and the human domain will be united, and the world will be made new. This is the day that we are all waiting for. The same day that Noah, Moses, Abraham, David, and everyone else in the Great Hall of Fame are waiting for. And it is happening, maybe not in our time, for the bible says no one knows the day or the hour, but there will be a new heaven and a new earth. My favorite part of these verses is "there shall be no mourning, nor crying, nor pain anymore.

As someone who has lived with chronic pain 24 hours a day, 7 days a week for almost 8 years, I can't wait for there to be no more crying and no more pain.

COME LORD JESUS!!!

I love the last book of the bible, it tells us that we win, well, we already won. It tells us that God will be dwelling with us permanently. A holy city will be built on the new earth, where God's people will worship him face to face. This city will be made of pure gold and jasper and its gates will be made of pearls. This is the end of this challenge, but hopefully the beginning of a whole new relationship with the LORD for you.

Memorize

"But the fruit of the Spirit is love, joy, peace, patience, kindness, goodness, faithfulness, gentleness, and self-control; against such things there is no law."

Galatians 5:22-24 ESV

Prayer

Lord, I love you and I love your word. Help me to fall more deeply in love with you and help me as I read today, to retain and understand what I am reading. I pray that you would speak to me through your word today and in this time of devotions.

About The Author

Suzanne Wright is a devoted Christian with over five decades of unwavering faith and more than 26 years of dedicated service in ministry. Her life's journey has been shaped by her deep-rooted commitment to God and her passion for sharing His word with others.

As a mother of three and a doting grandmother to six, Suzanne understands the importance of family and cherishes every moment spent with her loved ones. Her experiences as a parent and grandparent have enriched her perspective on life and faith, allowing her to connect with readers of all ages.

Suzanne's love for God's word is evident in her daily life and her writing. She finds immense joy and fulfillment in exploring the scriptures, constantly seeking to deepen her understanding and relationship with the Lord.

Currently, Suzanne volunteers her time in various capacities within her church community. She takes great pleasure in teaching home-schooled children, imparting not only knowledge but also valuable life lessons rooted in faith.

Through her writing, Suzanne aims to inspire, encourage, and guide readers on their own spiritual journeys. Her wealth of experience in ministry, combined with her relatable approach to faith and family, makes her work both insightful and accessible to Christians at all stages of their walk with God.

Written by Christyn Carter (daughter)

www.ingramcontent.com/pod-product-compliance
Lightning Source LLC
Chambersburg PA
CBHW071714120626
46550CB00001B/221